FOREWORD

I will start out this forward by warning you, dear reader, of the power you now hold in your hands. The words written in this book bare raw emotion, but at the same time demonstrate how to have a firm foundation in unstable seasons of your life. You can read this as a story, or you can put yourself in the midst of this family and allow your mind to go to a place of question and pain that may be uncomfortable. You have the power to allow the words in this book to bring healing to your grief. After you finish reading it, I encourage you to pass it on to someone you know who may also be dealing with the grieving process of death.

This is a coming of age tale. Luke Goodman, the son of the author Kim Goodman, is a young adventurous soul just on the cusp of manhood. Full of expectation for the future, his life ends tragically.

This book gives hope that the adventure is not over. There is life after death. More importantly, there can be joy after death.

I am a family friend of the Goodman's. I have watched their sons grow up: from running the kettle corn business to ministering on a stage in front of hundreds of people. A few weeks before Luke's death, I was talking to him in the parking lot at church. I always admired Luke - his supernatural athleticism and intellectual curiosity. I loved to watch people gasp when he would solve a Rubik's cube while on a pogo stick. Ha, who does that?!

While we were talking, I asked Luke, "So, what's next? I know you have graduated. You are talented in whatever you decide to do. So, what are you going to decide to do?" He just smiled, with his million-dollar grin and said, "Ya know, I've been seeking God a lot more. The cool thing about not knowing what is next, is that it forces you to completely rely on God and hang on for the ride...the adventure." His outlook was refreshing.

I thought about our conversation when I heard that he had gone to Heaven. He's on to the next adventure. Knowing Luke, he's probably playing Frisbee golf in Heaven, and out jumping all the angels while snowboarding down the black diamond slopes of Heaven's clouds.

There can be triumph in the midst of tragedy. Kim Goodman writes from her soul, but also from her faith. This book bears raw emotions but at the same time is lined up with the foundational truths of her faith. Whether or not you believe in God, we all have questions about death. Our mind wonders. These chapters unravel mysteries behind pain and show that inner healing can happen. This book is for anyone who has ever asked, "Why?"

Kim emphasizes in this book that God is not afraid of our

questions. She invites you to be a part of a family that puts God first, and lives life to the fullest despite not having all the answers. Kim and her family live by this motto, "We are all human with a touch of the divine." I love that! It reminds me that God's hand can always be at work in our lives.

Kim does not just tell you about grief and joy, she takes you on a journey with her. She welcomes you into her family portrait. Reading this book is like sharing family stories over a cup of coffee at Kim's kitchen counter late at night.

I lost my father to cancer, though he was a giant of faith. He was a man who believed in healing, but it did not happen for him. I had never really confronted questions that were going on in my mind. I just decided to believe in God and that He still works miracles despite my personal experience. Although things were left un-confronted, I thought my soul was healed. This book helped me deal with those questions that I never got answered. This book pushed me further into my walk with God. Even though this book is about death, it can also bring life. God is not afraid of our questions. Grief is necessary, but recovery is available.

John Daugherty, Creative Pastor for Victory and co-pastor of Victory downtown, Tulsa, OK; playwright and creative genius behind Victory's Broadway caliber Christmas and Easter productions.

WHAT PEOPLE ARE SAYING

"I had the wonderful privilege of being Kim's roommate in college. While I slept, she was up studying; at 5am, then classes, then more study until 12am—and I was still sleeping! She was the most disciplined and intentional person I had ever met. I always thought she would do something great with her life. Well... *Grace in Grief* is it! Kim and her remarkable family have navigated through the most harrowing experience anyone could find themselves, and yet, come out on the other side with hearts full of *real joy*. Kim opens her journal and reveals her own heart and soul-journey; vulnerably allowing us to walk with her through her darkest hours and deepest grieving, into wholeness and freedom. She teaches precious pearls of wisdom on how to connect with God when you can barely lift your eyes, and how He can transform your life through gratefulness—how to fill your soul when you are so dry, discouraged and empty from your own pain. She takes you to a deep place of inner healing and freedom which produces the fruit of joy. If you follow the wisdom inside these pages, it will profoundly change your life...joy guaranteed! Kim, I believe this is your masterpiece!"

—KATIE LUCE
Co-Founder of Teen Mania Ministries

"We have known Greg and Kim for over 30 years. We have always admired their faith and commitment to family. They simply do life well. We were eating at our favorite restaurant when we received the tragic news of their incredible loss. There are some moments in life that you never forget. A few weeks later we sat with them around our kitchen table. We shared in their pain, knowing there were no magic words that would bring understanding to the incomprehensible. What impressed us most was their courage. Greg and Kim wanted to open up their hearts and share their story. This book is the fruit of that. When we lost our beloved son in a car accident at age 17 we leaned into the strength of others. It was the only way we survived. There would be no greater gift to Greg and Kim, no finer tribute to their amazing son Luke than this book becoming a source of strength to you."

ROB AND LAURA KOKE
pastors and founders of Shoreline Church, Austin, TX

"Told with grace, honesty, and unapologetic transparency, Kim's book *Grace in Grief* will inspire and compel you to take a fresh look at where you place your hope. Kim unflinchingly writes of the tragic circumstances surrounding the death of her son Luke to legal, edible marijuana and reveals the journey of her family to find a refined peace in the midst of a painful, confusing season in their walk with God. For anyone on the Christian journey seeking to find answers to the challenges and chaos we sometimes face in this world, *Grace in Grief* will allow you to ask those questions we are sometimes afraid to ask, and will guide you to a deeper relationship with God. It's a must-read survival guide for navigating the tumultuous terrain between mortality and eternity."

JULIE LYLES CARR
best-selling author of *Raising an Original:*
Parenting Each Child According to their Unique
and God-Given Temperament,
host of *The Modern Motherhood Podcast* from Crista Media,
pastor at Life.Family

DEDICATION

TO JESUS, the anchor of my soul, for relentlessly pursuing me in love.

FOR MY INCREDIBLE HUSBAND GREG who loved me and lived this with me. Thank you for giving me space and time to write and share our experience. After 28 years of marriage, my heart still leaps within me every time you walk into a room. I am so incredibly grateful for you. You do so much behind the scenes to keep everything running smoothly in every area because you can do anything. You continually amaze me with your thoughtfulness and sweet sensitivity. You are a joy to do life with—with you there is never a dull moment. You have been such a great role model for our boys in being a great provider, entrepreneur, father, and husband. It is a privilege and honor to be your help meet and wife. I am crazy about you, and I thank God for you.

I am thankful for your fantastic sense of humor – you keep me (and everyone else) laughing!

~

TO JACEN DAVID, (24), now my oldest son on earth. I am so proud of you for following hard after Jesus. You came home from California with the vision to develop the sense of community you found out there. You have been intentional about developing friendships that are like "iron sharpening iron." You have sought that out, instilled the vision in others here and have now very much created that. I am so proud of you for surrounding yourself with friends that love Jesus as you do. I know the Father has gifted you with a great mind that you will use for His glory. I have been proud of you, watching you build your window cleaning and power washing business this year and persevering through the lean winter months when it was difficult getting started. You kept looking for ideas and coming at it from different angles, and now you have built a successful business. You are, like your dad, quite the entrepreneur, always coming up with new creative ideas. I pray the Lord continue to bless you abundantly with ideas that are God-sized ideas. You have already impacted lives for eternity, and I believe there will be many more lives you will have a generational impact on for the Kingdom.

~

ROBERT CHASE, (21), you are more like Jesus in loving others than almost anyone I know. You have taken the best of your dad and his people skills and have become such a lover of people. I have been so very proud to see you giving of yourself, pouring into the lives of others. You have been there for your Young Life guys and have brought such joy and inspiration into their lives to help them become more like Jesus. The Lord's favor is on you, and people are drawn to the Jesus in you. It has been a joy watching the passion you have for marketing as you flow with creativity and ideas. Like your granddad, you are an idea man. You have so many options before you. In every situation you walk into, you are a leader, whether or not you have the given title. You will lead many into the Kingdom of Heaven. This summer you have done missions work, business, and marketing in Zimbabwe and Brazil. I believe the ideas you bring to the organizations you work with will change the course of their destiny. You will meet people in Heaven 100 years from now that came out of poverty after the impact your team made in their community.

CHAD JOSEPH, (17), it has been a joy watching you grow from a boy to a man this past year. It happened right before our eyes. You mentioned your interest in learning to fly and within the week started ground pilot school. You asked about starting concurrent enrollment in your junior year of high school, and the next week started college classes. You applied yourself beautifully and rose to the top of your class. It is crazy to me that you are already flying an airplane, and I am really proud of you.

I have loved watching you get involved with youth and pull together friends for volleyball and other events. You have stepped
up this year. You are the hardest worker I know; you get that
from me. To anything you apply yourself to, you are such an
asset. You have been intentional in surrounding yourself with
others that love the Lord and are a good influence. I remember
my friend Charla saying about you years ago, "Chad has got it.
He is ready." You are solid, and I am proud of you.

SETH RYAN, (15), you have become quite social this past
year. You remind me of Rob. You hang out with a great group
of friends and cousins. You are witty, fun and much beloved.
You have so much going for you. You passed me up this year in
height and just kept right on going—over six inches so far this
year! You have a smile that melts me. I loved watching you and
Chad improve your tennis game this year and increase your skill
as players. It was great having you play doubles together and
learn to work together as teammates and brothers. Like Karen
Kingsbury spoke over her son, I pray you go to bed each night
in the upcoming years knowing that you did all you could to
prepare yourself for what the Lord has for you. You are blessed
with rooted and steady role models as brothers, going before
you, that you can learn from and who love you dearly. I am so
grateful you are our son.

JOY NATALIE, (11), you are my little joy! You delight my heart with how you rejoice in everything and squeal with glee over so many things. I love watching you dance with passion, elegance and grace. I am so proud of you with the dances you choreograph yourself and perform in our living room. I am glad you often share your gift in blessing others, because it is a gift. You are such a giver and always thinking of what you can do for others. You are my little songbird, consistently worshipping and singing Greatest Showman songs, of course. I am so grateful to have a daughter after all these sons. You are the most blessed little girl to have all these excellent brothers. I love how you flit from one person to another, cuddling and loving on all of us. You have your daddy's teasing personality, and you crack me up and melt my heart when you interact with him especially.

TO MY SISTER TONI, for her love, counsel, wisdom, and support. I cannot imagine walking out this life journey without you. I am so grateful to bounce everything off you throughout the years. You are one of the best communicators I know. You have imparted such parenting wisdom to me. You have done a phenomenal job with David, raising ten thriving children that will impact their generation in a mighty way. I am so thrilled about your book *Thrive* that is soon to come out. It will change lives, Toni. You truly know how to thrive, as does all of your family. Your book will rock the world.

TO MY MOM, my prayer warrior. Thank you for always being there for me. You inspire me. You are such a woman of faith. I thank you for all you have instilled in us in our love for Jesus. Thank you for the strong roots you put down for us in our growing up years. I know so much scripture because of what you had us learn in our growing up years. Thank you for the incredible example you have been as you have walked this most extenuating journey fighting cancer this year. You told the surgeon so many times, "No side effects! I am not going to have any side effects!" and you pretty much didn't. You are a rock, an anchor, and a beautiful soul. I love you.

AND TO ALL MY FRIENDS who loved me, came along beside me, and walked me through. I cherish your friendships. I am so grateful to do life with you all. I have gleaned such wisdom from all of you. I have the best girlfriends in the world, and you have all added so much joy and beauty to my life.

CONTENTS

PROLOGUE

MARCH 21, 2015

We were driving home to Tulsa, OK after a fantastic family snowboarding trip to Vail, CO. We had spent a glorious week together with four of our six kids, sharing laughter and fun on the slopes. I was talking with my husband Greg on the way home and telling him how grateful I was for our family. "I love the relationships we share with our adult children. I love our family. We are so incredibly, richly blessed."

We had left our oldest son Luke, who was 22, at a bus stop that morning. He was going to make a bus connection and join his cousins, who were some of his best friends, for another five days of snowboarding. He was doing what he loved best with some of his favorite people in the world.

We got into Tulsa around eight that evening. Later that night as we were sleeping we got a phone call from the police. "You need to let us in the gate." Bewildered and dazed from sleep,

Greg and I went out and sat on the porch swing to talk with them as they arrived.

"We got a call from Summit County."

Greg gasped. Nothing registered with me as I was not aware of where Summit County was at that moment.

"We got a call saying that your son Luke has been shot in the right temple."

"Oh my God!" I cried. "What happened?!!" The thought never crossed my mind that Luke could have pulled the trigger.

"They are suspecting that it is a self-inflicted gunshot wound to the head."

INTRODUCTION

This book is for everyone who has known loss. Grief and loss have many faces; the woman in her 50's who finds herself divorced after 28 years of marriage. The man who lost his mother, wife, and daughter all within minutes due to a tragic car wreck. The cohesive, loving family whose son took his life soon after graduating college, when his family had such high hopes for him. The man who loses the job he has faithfully worked for decades, just before he is fully qualified for his pension. The young girl who witnessed her 6-year-old sister run over and killed by a delivery truck driver. The young man who accidentally ran over his precious sister, after she saw his car and ran out to greet him. The mother who lost her unborn baby due to miscarriage. The mother who chose to abort her baby, thereby ending the life inside her. Losing a mom, who was a lifetime best friend, to cancer after a long-fought battle and endless doctor visits. Watching a dad wither away to 100 pounds in his fight with cancer. Losing a mother-in-law to Alzheimer's when it feels like she is gone, even when she is still with you. Losing the grandmother you loved so dearly, who sincerely believed in you. Watching a younger 21-year-old sister get out of the shower, and collapse on the floor because she cannot get the oxygen she needs to breathe because of the disease ravaging her body.

This book is for the teenager that has been molested since she was a young child. The girl abducted into human trafficking that has lost all hope. The young man in his twenty's that does cutting in his desperation. The female that is bulimic because of her low self-image. All of these have experienced deep loss. This book is to bring hope. Although my story is different, the principles are life-changing.

Some have witnessed gruesome deaths of their loved ones; the high-school girl huddling in fear in a closet, in her art class at Santa Fe High School. The shooter fired bullets into the closet as he yelled out profanities, killing two of her classmates and splattering their blood on her body. The entire student body faces devastation and loss in light of the many other students randomly murdered that day. The students that lost ten friends that day. The young man, newly married to the love of his life that within a month of moving with her into their brand-new home, that had a drunk driver run his truck through their bedroom one night, while they were sleeping, rolling his bride in their mattress and suffocating her to death.

Loss of any kind can lead to grief. It can come in any number of forms. We all face grief over the course of our lives in hundreds of different ways, both small and large. I wrote this book after the most consuming grief I have ever had to face—the loss of my oldest son after he pulled the trigger at 22 years of age and ended his beautiful life. Devastating loss: like waves in an ocean that threaten to consume. Like a tsunami.

Losing my son was the fifth time an immediate family member of mine crossed over into Heaven. My sister went to be with Jesus at 21 when I was 23. My beloved dad followed her eleven years later after a battle with esophageal cancer. I miscarried two daughters that joined them in Heaven. Each of their deaths has left me with an eternal perspective I did not have before. We tend to become so caught up in the here and now. The Lord has such an eternal perspective that we do not have. Heaven seems a little closer and a little sweeter with each family member that relocates there. After my son Luke went to Heaven, I have come away with the realization that relationships are all we take with us. Relationships: pouring into, sowing into, and loving others are the things that matter most in this life.

No two people experience the same loss, just as no two people grow up in the same family. I had to deal with my two sisters, and they had to deal with me. I saw things from my perspective; they saw things from theirs. When my dad passed away, my sister and I eulogized him. We had two radically different ways in which we viewed my dad. Neither wrong nor right; just unique. We each processed in our own way, in our own timing. This book is intended to share my journey. I knew I wanted to emerge from this great loss whole. I wanted the same for my big, beautiful family. I share with you my journey in the hope that it will help you in yours, that you gain insights that help you emerge whole as well.

In raising our six children (all from one wonderful husband), we have always taken advantage of sharing object lessons. We can learn from the experiences, failures, and successes of others and apply those same principles to our own life. Learning from others can help us navigate those landmines and hopefully avoid them in our own lives. It is my hope and prayer that my story will do that for you. Your loss is different than mine, even if it is the same scenario, because of the way you uniquely process it. My intention is that you are able to take away insights that help you as you journey through your loss to wholeness.

I started this book a year after losing my son. It has now been three years. It is a journey. Life happens in the meantime. Distractions have gotten in the way of my writing. In places of the book, I refer to the amount of time that has passed, and that may seem to jump around. I leave it because it matters to the thought process at that time.

In this book, I draw from many sources. No man is an island. We all impact and are impacted by those around us. I continuously fill my soul with rich writings, with words that bring life. I share many of these with you, from a plethora of sources, because they impacted me on my journey to wholeness and healing. My prayer is that they minister to you as they did me.

"Nobody Ever Died from Marijuana"

"Death changes us, the living. In the presence of death, we become more aware of life. It can inspire us to decide what really matters in life – and then to seek it."

Candy Lightner, *Giving Sorrow Words*

Luke and Jace both started college at Oral Roberts University together in the fall of 2010. Luke was eighteen, Jace was only sixteen. I had homeschooled the kids since Luke was three. Jace was always very academically gifted, so I began schooling them together from the time Jace was in kindergarten and Luke was in second grade. As a result, Jace always felt "misplaced" in sports, and was young socially with others in his same grade. I would not do it again if I had it to do over; that is, I would not have moved him ahead because he was so bright academically. I would definitely homeschool again. It has been an honor and a privilege to teach my children and to spend

7

countless hours with them over the years doing so.

My degree was in nursing. I was an ICU nurse, a transplant nurse, and an Organ Donor Coordinator. It was not my intention to homeschool my kids. My husband and I decided we would like to lay a good, strong foundation for our children's lives. When Luke was three, I started with a group of friends in the Houston area. We began with just one day a week and loved it. Luke homeschooled until his junior year in high school and then chose to complete his schooling in public school. Jace homeschooled through high school and did concurrent enrollment during his senior year, so he was able to start ORU with 26 credit hours under his belt.

By the time Jace got to college, we had discussed with him whether he wanted to wait a year and have other pursuits. He decided to head straight into college. Because we had homeschooled, he had been sheltered in his upbringing. His roommate his freshman year was from Colorado where marijuana had already been legalized. So, we homeschool our son from kindergarten through high-school, send him off to a Christian college, and the first week he is introduced to marijuana by his roommate. He was so young at sixteen to be off on his own and was easily influenced. He succumbed to peer pressure.

Meanwhile, Luke was introduced to pot through waitstaff peers at a restaurant where he had been working in high school. Neither Luke nor Jace smoked it regularly; both did socially on rare occasions.

We first found out about it during their sophomore year of

college. My husband Greg and I had them both come home the next night, and we had them join us in our bedroom to watch the movie "Flight." In the movie, Denzel Washington plays a commercial airline pilot who is a raging alcoholic. He attempts to cover his addiction. The movie powerfully portrays the consequences of his addiction—it destroys him and sucks the life out of him. When the movie was over, we turned off the television, looked at Luke and Jace, and said, "Do you have anything that you want to tell us?"

We allowed it to get painfully quiet in the room as the realization dawned on them that they had been found out, and they were busted. We talked for the next two and a half hours. For Jace, it was a relief to have been found out. He wanted and needed to quit, and he needed the accountability and the challenge not to smoke pot again. He decided to quit that night, and he did.

For Luke, it was different. He rationalized, cajoled, and attempted to reason with us. He justified, "No one has ever died from marijuana." He argued that for him it was a "spiritual" experience. He and his cousin would smoke together, and then they would get into deep theological discussions. He felt it opened his mind to see things more deeply than he had before. Luke left that night making the decision in his heart to "try" to quit, not with a definitive decision to stop smoking.

I had never smoked pot. I had never taken a puff of anything. I honestly only knew what I had read about marijuana. I knew it was considered a "gateway" drug—one that could eventually lead a user into harder drugs to get the same high that they would from pot. It causes a person to become less concerned about life in general. It made my sons much more apathetic in their studies.

Luke and I had always had a close relationship. Until his senior year of high school and his first couple of years of college, he shared his heart and soul with me. During those years he kept his struggles to himself.

We have a kettle corn business that we work together as a family. Eleven years ago, Greg saw the set up for sale on Craigslist and decided it would be a good business experience for the boys. They have grown up with it. Rob was only ten when he began working with us and was asking if he could cook by the time he was eleven. Jace is 28 months older than Rob. We have had a blast working together as a family over the years. I love listening to Luke, Jace, and Rob bantering with one another as they work. They are hilarious, and like their Dad, their humor is not at another person's expense. We recently had five events going on simultaneously in five different cities over one weekend. It has been a huge financial blessing, as well as an incredible business learning experience for the kids. They get to hire their friends, and see the difference between being a business owner and an employee. So basically, the first two years they were at ORU, the only time we saw Luke and Jace was when we worked kettle corn events together.

Luke's passion growing up, unfortunately, was video games. From the time he was ten, he filled countless hours playing them. As parents, we tried to put a limit on how much of the kids' time could be spent on video games, but Luke and even Jace both would violate that. One hour a day turned to five. "Only on weekends" grew into whenever they could sneak it in.

We all make choices in our lives. The kind of food we choose to eat every day will eventually determine how we look, our health, and our energy level. Rob made an intentional decision at thirteen. He watched his older brothers waste their lives and time playing video games and decided he was going to do something productive with his life instead. He used those hours to teach himself to play guitar. The choice he made has opened up countless opportunities for him. He became involved in leading worship for his youth group. That led to relationships with countless amazing people.

Luke chose video games. He became one of the top players in the world in his favorite one, *League of Legends*. To be among the top in the world means a lot of time spent. Luke began to battle guilt over wasting his time and his life playing video games. We have a real enemy, Satan, that is looking for a way, any way, to get a foothold in our lives and rob us of our potential. For Luke this was video games. The enemy of our souls beat Luke up and made him feel worthless.

When Luke went off to college for his freshman year, he insisted on having his own room. Who does that in college?! The whole point of living on campus is to assimilate with others, make new friends, and get to be a part of the culture. Unknown to Greg and me, his reason was that he did not want to have to answer to anyone about the time he spent on video games.

Nine months after he died, we found a letter he had left on his computer. It had been locked, and Rob had unlocked it when he was home for break and needed to use a computer. Luke wrote it during a time in his freshman year that was one of the lowest points in his life, admitting in it that he was completely addicted to video games. Luke wanted to break the cycle and did not know how. He would stay up till three in the morning playing and then drag himself to class the next day. Even in class, all he could think about was getting back to his games. He lamented how worthless he felt as a result and considered ending his life because of it.

There is an entire generation that is being robbed by their addiction to video games. I recently heard about an eighth grader that hanged himself over the guilt and worthlessness he felt over his addiction to video games. I have seen five-year-olds sit and play for two hours, completely unaware of their surroundings and engrossed in their games. Another man I know was very addicted to them through his teenage years. When he got married, he would stay up all hours of the night playing them. His marriage ended in divorce. A friend of the family told me that in college, when one new game came out, the campus was like a ghost town the whole week—all the guys were playing in their rooms. Playing video games is a choice. Playing them in disobedience to rules set by parents is yet another choice. One choice leads to another, and choices have consequences.

After we found Luke's letter, Jace shared that video games

suck the life out of their captives. He said, "You can't play video games without them draining the life out of you. I got three to four years down the road, and realized all my friends had moved on in life and I was stuck." Jace decided to quit playing video games so he could get on with his life and all that God had in store for him.

The Lord has given every one of us a moral compass. Whether or not something has been forbidden by parents, we know in our hearts that we are not pleasing the Lord by wasting the time and talents that He has given us. He calls us all to be good stewards of the gifts we have. Matthew 25:14-30 tells the parable of the good steward. In it, a man is going on a long trip. Before leaving he gives five talents to one of his servants, two to another, and one to the last, according to their abilities. When the man returns, the first two have both doubled what he had given them. The master praises them and awards them even greater responsibilities. The third instead had buried his talents in the ground. Sounds a lot like wasting time on meaningless activities like video games. The master calls him a wicked servant and gives his portion to the first. He then says, "To everyone who has more will be given, and he will have an abundance; but from the one who does not have even what he has will be taken away. And throw out the worthless servant into the outer darkness; in that place there will be weeping and grinding of teeth.

About three months after Luke died, I was journaling about how, for the first time since he died, I was mad at him. I was disappointed that he had wasted thousands of hours of his time playing video games when he could have been doing productive things: using his talents, ministering to others, sowing into his younger sibling's lives, connecting with their hearts. I felt the bad choices Luke made in his life were selfish. He was not considering that what he did could affect others who were watching him. My brother-in-law David has said, "Our attitude affects everyone and everything in our environment." I would add to that, what we do with our lives affects everyone and everything in our environment. That makes us want to stop and take inventory of how we are living. What am I doing today, and how is that going to impact others?

We had a manhood ceremony for Rob recently, when he reached adulthood. That evening Bruno Teles, a professor who has profoundly impacted Rob's life, said to Rob, "Never miss an opportunity to impact another's life." What a way to live! Our attitudes, choices, and the way we choose to live out our lives can have tremendous repercussions, even eternally, on the lives of others. Our choices do matter!

When Luke died, he was not the same person that had struggled years before. He had grown tremendously in life and in his walk with the Lord. His smile lit up a room. He had this easy-going way about him. He was the one at a party that would seek out the person off by himself, draw him in, and make him feel included. Luke had started working out six days a week, mostly with his buddy Ethan. He was muscular and good-looking. Luke looked like a movie star. He hung around friends that sharpened his character, as "Iron sharpens iron." He consciously decided to stop playing video games, and he too decided to pick up the guitar and learn to play. He would sing his heart out. His brothers and cousins joke that Luke was never afraid to hit the high notes. He was full of joy, love, and adventure.

He was a lover of life. He was a daredevil on a snowboard. During our last week with him in Vail, he and I were going down the slope together. He was wearing only his Kevin Durant jersey with his muscular bare arms, his lit-up lime green pants, and his blue reflective ray bans. Some girl had asked him for his autograph for wearing the Durant jersey his previous run. Luke was turning circles on his snowboard in front of me the whole time going down the slope while carrying on a conversation with me, his gorgeous grin lighting up my life. I joked, "That girl is going to want *your* autograph now after watching you—forget Kevin Durant!"

He could do anything on a board of any kind; whether it was a longboard, surfboard, wakeboard or wake surf board. He was amazing, like his dad, on a ski. Although I do have to say, no one comes close to Greg on a ski—he is really incredible and makes it look like art. Luke also loved disc golf. I am always the cheerleader that just walks along with the rest of the family while Greg, Luke, Jace, Rob, Chad, and Seth all make their fabulous disc golf throws. I love watching them perform and compete with one another.

Nine months before Luke died he had an experience where the Lord challenged him and warned him against smoking pot. He came to me and said, "Mom, in the story about Adam and

Eve in the Garden when the Lord warned them not to eat from the tree of the Knowledge of Good and Evil, the tree could have been Cannabis." He talked about how it put people's minds on a different plane spiritually and how the Lord did not want them to go there. Other times when he smoked pot, he would experience a terrifying darkness. The Lord showed him he was to stay away from it. The Lord often spoke to him through dreams, and He had several dreams that confirmed this conviction.

Satan masquerades as light. What Luke felt was an intense spiritual experience from smoking pot was really Satan's counterfeit. He hungered for relationship and intimacy with the Father, and at times felt like he found it through marijuana. True intimacy with the Father comes from being still in His Presence and listening to Him. He says in Psalms 46:10, "Be still and know that I am God." He is always speaking to us if we will still our hearts before Him and listen for His voice.

> *He is always speaking to us if we will still our hearts before Him and listen for His voice.*

I was not aware that eight months after Luke's heartfelt commitment to not use marijuana that he began rationalizing within himself and had smoked again once in February, before our trip in March. Now It was back on his radar. When we dropped him off at the bus stop that morning, there was a dispensary on the street corner where you could buy marijuana legally. Luke had brought his gun on the trip, unbeknownst to my husband and me. Luke knew ahead of time he was going to need to make this bus connection, so he brought it for safety reasons, as my husband often has when we've traveled.

The seed was planted when he saw the dispensary. He met up with his cousin, whom he had smoked with in the past. His cousin had been snowboarding with his girlfriend's family. That same day they took the bus together back to the dispensary. They were curious and wanted to try marijuana edibles—marijuana-laced candy or food such as cookies or brownies. Taking marijuana edibles is not the same as smoking pot. Who eats just one piece of candy? After they had one edible, they waited 45 minutes or so, but they did not feel a thing. When a person smokes pot, the effects are felt almost immediately. They decided to have another candy. Another thirty minutes went by, and still they felt nothing. Ultimately, Luke consumed five edibles in a two-hour period before he began realizing any effects.

An acquaintance of ours, a grown man with a family of his own, told us he had been curious to try edibles when he was in Colorado the previous year. He ate one. The effects of it were crazy. He said if he had a gun, he would have shot himself. The woman at the car rental place we used on our trip told us she had tried one when she moved there and was flat out on the floor for two days.

Luke's cousin and his girlfriend were headed to the hot tub to join her family before it closed in ten minutes. He said Luke was not in his right mind. He was "talking out of his head." He was totally under the influence of marijuana and not making any sense at all. His cousin had never seen him like this before

17

and felt like the best thing would be to just let him "diffuse" for a while. They left to join the others at the hot tub. His girlfriend's mom, a police officer, passed by them as they were heading down, as she was heading back to the room where they were staying at the condo. Within a minute of her return, she heard a gunshot and hit the floor. It had not been five minutes since his cousin left him when he pulled the trigger.

We all can see how the enemy of our souls brings condemnation. Because of the over the top overdose of marijuana, Luke was not in his right mind. Satan condemned him, and Luke bought into the lies. We have all bought into Satan's lies. Jesus never condemns. Never! He convicts and He corrects. He never condemns. We have to learn to recognize the lies and choose to walk in His truth instead; to believe in His deep, incredible love for us.

A dear friend of our entire family, Amy, wrote a letter to the dispensary where Luke and his cousin purchased the edibles:

"I want to introduce you to Luke Goodman. He was a 22-year old young man who loved life. He was a December university graduate and seeker of adventure. Luke may be the only person you would have ever met who could ride a pogo stick and simultaneously solve a very confused Rubik's cube in less than 45 seconds! He was the best at every sport he ever tried. Luke was the oldest of 6 kids; five boys, and the youngest, a girl. His little sister adored him. He was homeschooled and was

a friend to all he met. Luke had ten cousins, all from the same family, that lived across the street. They did everything together. They boarded, water skied, biked, built forts, camped, and did life together every day for all the years of their lives. They had been an extension of each other since they were little. He was on this trip to Keystone with one cousin and awaiting two others. They valued family above all else.

Luke had never suffered from depression or been treated for any kind of mental issue. He was looking forward to the next stage of his life having just grad-uated. He had a new workout routine with his cousin. He had made specific plans for the upcoming week and for when he returned home to Tulsa, Oklahoma. He couldn't wait to spend time with his family in Colo-rado and then spend some days with his best friends, his cousins, for four days after his mom and dad and siblings left. He had everything to look forward to and a rich and beautiful life to live.

Luke decided to try recreational and legal marijua-na, which he bought from your store, while in Keystone on this trip. He took too much candy and within a couple of short hours became verbally unclear, glassy-eyed and presented as having some hallucinogenic ide-ations. In less than five minutes of being left alone, he was mentally tormented and took his life. Luke did NOT commit suicide. Suicide is a choice made by a person deciding that they no longer want to reside in this world. Luke desperately wanted to stay here, to laugh with his family and hang with his cousins, brothers, family, and friends. He would be devastated by what happened . . . if he could understand. He would be crushed to see his little sister grieving for her big brother, his cousins, and brothers in tears because their days of making memories with him are over; his beautiful mother kissing the dimple on the left side of his face which she had kissed so many times, and grieving because the last time she kissed it was the last time she would see him so full of life and happy. His beautiful dad, strong and manly, weeping at his bedside. Luke, in his full senses, would NEVER have chosen this. He was too happy and had too much going for him. This was 100% the psychotic break his brain experienced from ingesting too much THC.

It is important for you to "know" this young man. It's important for you to know that because of the far-reaching relationships and influence this large family had, that tonight there are hundreds, if not thousands, of people, grieving, mourning, and numb with grief. From Thailand, where his lifetime best friend resides, to South Africa where another close friend lives, to the west and east coast, people are in deep grief and shock. He was much loved. He will be missed forever. Our lives are changed . . . forever.

We are believers in personal responsibility and accountability. We know Luke was twenty-two and responsible for his own choices. We also believe that lacing sugar candy with drugs and expecting people to "only take the recommended dose" is unrealistic and a highly inflammatory statement. We have an obesity problem in this country partly because rarely can people say "no" to sugar. Sugar is as addictive as a drug, and now you are mixing the two. This is now being offered to anyone over the age of eighteen, even though their brains are not yet fully developed until they are twenty-five. While I still hold these young people ultimately responsible for their actions you are not completely exempt from your part in this senseless and tragic death. Colorado is not exempt. If we had voted differently, if people had more respect for the fragility of life, Luke would still be here.

I shared Luke with you because if I didn't, you may go home tonight and wipe his name from your thoughts and go about your life as if this did not matter. I want you to think about his beautiful little sister grieving for her brother, and his mother holding his hand and kissing his face over and over in the hospital waiting for them to come and take him off life support. We had to, and have to, live this out every day for the rest of our lives. You don't get to walk away without any modicum of understanding of the part you and your specific dispensary played in the tragedy. God forgive us as a state and nation for offering, with so little thought, enticements that can be so deadly.

Thank you for taking the time to read my tribute to our precious Luke Goodman."

AMY GLEASON BIRD

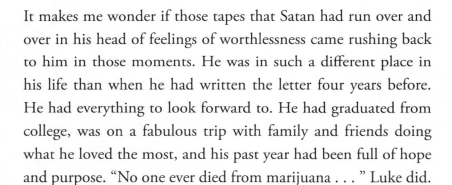

It makes me wonder if those tapes that Satan had run over and over in his head of feelings of worthlessness came rushing back to him in those moments. He was in such a different place in his life than when he had written the letter four years before. He had everything to look forward to. He had graduated from college, was on a fabulous trip with family and friends doing what he loved the most, and his past year had been full of hope and purpose. "No one ever died from marijuana . . . " Luke did.

LUKE

Hundreds of people responded with heartfelt words about Luke on Facebook after he died. His memorial service packed out the church to standing room only. A friend sent us a picture of the traffic backed up on the freeway with people trying to get to the service. He was incredibly, dearly loved by many. It was because he loved so well. He had an infectious joy. Luke had this easy way about him that made you slow down and savor the moment.

At his memorial service, my husband Greg had the brilliant idea of wanting to portray a visual of Luke. We had several of our favorite pictures of him blown up to poster-board size to display up front. Across the platform, we placed all the things Luke excelled at and loved. His wakeboard, snowboard, longboard, wakesurf board, pogo stick, bowling ball, Rubik's cube, stilts, Frisbee, disc golf Frisbees, Ping-Pong paddle, and other reminders all lined the front.

I had been to funerals where the Lord was so glorified, and people left inspired. I wanted Luke's service to be that way. Our large family, my sister's large family, and my mom (who is widowed) walked out together down the center aisle and joined hands together across the stage. It was a powerful statement of unity.

A friend of mine had given me the verse Genesis 50:20 where, after Joseph had been sold into slavery by his brothers, he said to them, "As for you, you meant evil against me, but God meant it for good, that many people may be kept alive, as they are this day." The Lord had used their intended evil against him in his life to serve His purpose in Joseph's life. Joseph became a slave to Potiphar, one of the leaders of Egypt. He had the Lord's favor on him and was trusted by Potiphar to run his affairs until Potiphar's wife wrongly accused him of molesting her after he refused to sleep with her. Joseph was then thrown into jail.

Joseph remained faithful in his heart and life. He had the Lord's continued favor on him. He correctly interpreted dreams the Pharaoh's butcher and baker had while they were in prison. Later, when Pharaoh had a prophetic dream, Joseph was called to make sense of it, released from jail, and ultimately became the right-hand man to Pharaoh. He became the brains of the operation preparing for drought in the land of Egypt. Because of him, many were kept alive.

The Lord brought such redemption in Joseph's life. We are believing He will bring redemption in Luke's death. In my intro, I mentioned the Santa Fe shootings that happened in late May of 2018. The same young man whose wife was rolled into the mattress and suffocated was a dear friend of our family, Bobby Petrocelli. His wife was my sister Toni's best friend, Ava. Bobby affectionately called her "Avala." She was an absolute joy and gift to all who knew her. Bobby was crazy about her. He adored her. He wrote a book, *Triumph Over Tragedy*, in which he tells his story. He is a gifted writer, and his book will take you on such a roller coaster of emotions. From there, he became a motivational speaker. His theme became "30-second decisions," how they can impact and change the course of our lives. He has gone on to write motivational books such as *You Matter, It Doesn't*. Bobby was a misplaced New Yorker and the football coach at Santa Fe High School back in the mid 80s after graduating college. He loved the students there. They and his wife were his life.

The student body adored Bobby. When Ava was killed, they rallied around him like you have never seen. There were over 2,000 people at her funeral, and the majority of them were his students. He poured into their lives, and they poured back into his when he lost his wife. Fast-forward almost forty years and inconceivable tragedy strikes this same Santa Fe High School. A raging shooter destroys and ends the lives of ten students, injuring ten more. Bobby still has a heart for the students there. He spoke to an auditorium of students and parents and ministered to them in the wake of their shock and tragedy. He too had known deep pain, heart-wrenching suffering and he related to their distress. He ministered grace and healing. Redemption. Restoration. He has given students new focus, new purpose. The

Lord doesn't waste anything. Forty years later he is using Bobby to reach the hearts and souls of students that could otherwise have been lost. He brings those kids the message of God's love and hope, giving them a reason to go on living.

We have prayed and believed Luke's untimely death would be a warning to many, so that they too would not succumb to the temptation of edibles. That they would recognize it is a lie of the enemy to rationalize that it is ok to use marijuana occasionally. As for Satan, he meant evil in leading Luke to take his life, but the Lord is going to use Luke's death for good, that many people would be kept alive as they are this day. We pray his story may prevent others from making the same mistake with marijuana. His death has served as a warning, an awakening. It has given many an awareness of the danger in the complacency of this generation. "There is a way that seems right to a man and appears straight before him, but its end is the way of death." (Proverbs 16:25) I would not want another mother, another father, or another family to have to walk through the pain of losing their loved one as we have.

It seems like the lines are fuzzier between right and wrong in the millennial generation than they were when I was growing up. More young people experiment with marijuana, even on a Christian campus. We had calls from the media all across the nation regarding Luke's death under the influence of edibles. His story went from coast to coast, and as far as to the United Kingdom. It raised awareness. Our prayer was that lives would be impacted and people would make an intentional choice to not use marijuana because of his death. As a result, many have committed not to touch it again.

Meg Jennings, a friend of Luke's, wrote on his Facebook wall the day of the service:

"Today was a reminder that God is a good God and that God is a faithful God. Luke Goodman, it was a privilege to get to know you over the past few years. You and your brothers are the most jovial people I know. You were an encouragement to many, and from the looks of the packed house this morning, you will continue to be that for all those whose hearts you touched. You were a breath of fresh air, and with that, you challenged us all to be the same for those around us. Thank you for passing along your joy and allowing God to invest in you so that you would be able to invest in others. We will miss you dearly."

Aba Hammond wrote of Luke, "Luke was full of life. His smile was one of a kind. If you were in a bad mood and he smiled at you, you would automatically smile back. He always put others before himself. He was humble. He loved the Lord. He lived a life that exemplified the story of God's amazing grace. He led by example. When I attended the memorial service for Luke yesterday, I entered the church with a heavy heart. I was not smiling. I kept asking in my head "Why Luke?" But then the service started, and one by one people got up and spoke about what Luke meant to every one of them. I looked around the room and saw how full the room was to the point where people were standing. Luke had impacted every single person's life, not to mention people that couldn't make it and expressed their thoughts and wishes on the internet. At the end of the service, I had so much peace in my heart. Luke's family had fixed their eyes on the author and finisher of our faith. They were still standing. His family was celebrating the life that he lived, not glorifying the way that he had passed. That in itself was a beautiful thing to see and experience. When I say that Luke lived—I am not exaggerating. He probably did more than 70% of the things that are on my bucket list. He could solve a Rubik's cube while jumping on a pogo stick for the love of Christ. Consider my mind officially blown.

To the Goodman, Fowler, and Brock (his lifetime best friend) families, my heart grieves with you, but it also rejoices because he is with our Father now. God bless every one of you.

Luke, I miss you. I will never understand why your life was cut short, but I find solace in the fact that you are with our Father probably playing ping pong with Jesus. Death is not the greatest loss in life. You lived a fulfilling life, and Christ was evident in the way you portrayed yourself. And now, bask in His glory. Till we meet again at Jesus' feet."

Aba, your words were beautiful. I think someone's words are often much of a reflection of who they are, as much as about the person they are talking. I loved her line about "he lived a life that exemplified the story of God's amazing grace." We are all such recipients of God's amazing grace. I grew up in a Christian home. I was taught to understand that a person that committed suicide did not go to heaven. I stopped believing that years ago. I have personally read the entire Bible through many times. I have never come across a scripture to support that. We serve a God of love and grace. He is a God of judgment, and we are to fear Him reverentially, but he is also a God of mercy and grace.

Luke used to come in around eleven in the morning after I was well into my school day with his younger siblings. He would sit down beside me, with his slow, easy manner, and catch up on the previous day and let me know about the day ahead of him. His smile never failed to move me. I sincerely felt like it was a gift to have him living at home.

As a family, we have made it a high priority to have dinner together whenever possible. Through all the years of sports, kettle corn, youth group, and the many other demands on our time, we almost always sit down to dinner together. I loved seeing his face across from me at the table. He and his siblings have continually brought such life and light to our lives in just being together. Now that he is no longer with us, I will be eternally grateful for that time. I loved the times of heart-to-heart sharing we had. Like his dad and most of his siblings, he had such a quick wit. He never failed to make me smile and laugh. His absence has left such a hole in our lives.

Before Luke was declared brain dead, a very precious friend of our family went to the prayer tower at ORU, as she was a student there. She spent six hours crying and praying and believing God for his life. She said that Jesus then spoke to her and told her no. He said, "I asked Luke if he wanted to come back." Wow. I did not doubt that Luke was with Jesus because I knew his heart. But it was an incredible comfort hearing those words. Luke loved life. He lived it to the fullest. He was loved and adored by countless friends and family. Heaven is so incredible that given a choice, he wanted to stay there. He knew all he was leaving behind, and that the Lord was willing to let him live if that was what he wanted. Heaven is what we are living for on earth. We are living and walking with our Savior and wanting to know Him and make Him known so that one day we can spend eternity with Him. And Luke is already there. For that, I am eternally grateful. I miss him like crazy. My heart aches for him and yearns for him, but I will get to be with him for eternity.

> Heaven is so incredible that given a choice, he wanted to stay there.

I want to share with you a snapshot from my journal I wrote to Luke several months after he passed away. My thoughts are jumbled, but I just wrote what came to mind.

"Luke,

I miss you. I miss your essence. I miss your love. Your hugs. Your embrace. I miss kissing your soft, sweet dimple that I have kissed a thousand times. You had never grown man hairs yet on your cheeks—your entire life they stayed sweet as a baby's. I miss your smell. I miss cuddling you. Laying on the bed in the back of the motorhome and talking, you sharing your heart, your passions.

Oh, the layers of our lives. On the day you were born they whisked you out of my arms and rushed you to the ICU, there was meconium in the amniotic fluid. Later Daddy wheeled me all the way to Children's Hospital to hold you. The baby next to you coded, and they grabbed you out of my arms and threw us out. We cried all the way back. You nursed beautifully. Oh, how I loved you! I remember conversations with you in our Kansas house. With you, I would talk things out. You were always wise, even as a little child. We were always connected.

We took you camping, water skiing, rock climbing, and rollerblading as a baby. We were building the Amway business and would take you to a different house with us, night after night. I would put you down in a back bedroom in your car seat, and you would go right off to sleep. When you would wake up in your crib, you never fussed for me to come to get you. You would talk and babble—for up to an hour if it took that long for me to get you. You were always content.

I remember you and Daddy playing 'ball in the hall' in our Hatton Street house. Simple life. Hours in the park with friends. I remember you staying up all night to build a playset with Daddy one night in the backyard. We moved about six weeks later and had to leave the massive, wonderful swing-set there.

I remember your Galveston birthday party when you turned four and Jace turned two, (with sixty friends of the family). You were always precious, content, happy, well adjusted.

There was the time you and Daddy were horse-playing. You were about three and stood up on the couch, while he was throwing a pillow to you, and you were catching it and laughing hysterically. The next toss caught you off balance, and you fell over backward and landed on your head. You went limp like a noodle, and your pupils dilated 100 percent. It scared me so badly. I rode in the ambulance with you. Thank you, Father God, that he recovered completely.

Heelies. He wore those for years. One Heelie out, the other closed for the longest time. He bought his first pair of Heelies with the well-earned money he saved for months and months. $100! He was so proud of his first major purchase to buy them. He used to get so many double takes from people admiring his speed and agility on his Heelies once he figured out how to use both wheels. He did the same thing with rollerblades. One tennis shoe, one rollerblade. He dreamed one night that he could rollerblade, he was working it out in his sleep. That gave him the confidence he needed and the next day he put rollerblades on both feet, and off he went—with much confidence. Then when he learned to ride a bike, he did the same thing. He dreamed he could, which allowed him to get over his fears, and the next morning he hopped on his bike and rode away.

I used to rollerblade for miles in the morning around our home in Kansas. Our house was one of fourteen in a circle around a pond. Luke would just come out and wait for me on the next lap when the kids needed me. Greg had a 3 ½ foot remote boat he ran on the pond there. We would watch together with delight as it gained crazy speed zipping across the water. We set up obstacle courses in the playground there, and the neighbors would join in with our boys competing for the fastest finish. Greg and Luke went to the field across the street in their cute matching aqua shirts and khaki shorts and flew Greg's extreme kite, with two strings to control the zipping and zagging, as it wildly raced through the air.

All the moves. We moved homes eight times in three years. While living at his grandparent's bay house in Galveston, Luke would throw the fishing net for hours on end, never tiring of the next surprise in his catch. I could only make a tangled mess of it at best. We would feed the seagulls from the upstairs porch, throwing bread out as they circled and caught it in the air. We would play at what we named the 'castle park', playing hide and seek, or the game where you had to jump from place to place without ever allowing your feet to touch the actual ground as we raced to tag one another.

Then there was the lady at the laundromat. We never saw her smile; she seemed very unhappy. We determined over the course of our summer there to bring joy into her life. We would bring little treats to her. We took flowers. We prayed for her. We watched her soften her hard facade; we chipped away at it with each visit. Our final stop by she hugged us and held back tears. She was one of the highlights of our summer.

Beach times. Rollerblading for miles on the seawall with Luke.

Boat times. All through the years. Greg taught water skiing when I first met him. He had a 'boom' that he could attach, sticking out from the middle of the boat, to teach people to get the feel of skiing before letting them loose in the back of the boat. He taught me to slalom that way. Once on the boom, once with a rope five feet off the boom, and then first time up off the back. Luke, Jace, Rob and their cousins used to love to 'drag' on the boom. No ski, just hold on for dear life. It was quite hilarious watching them. Luke would be behind the boat on the kneeboard just singing away, talking non-stop. I never, ever tire of watching the kids and their antics behind the boat. He would come to sit by me and cuddle up as we then watched his brothers.

Years of playing games in the evenings with the family—Luke never stopping making noises as we played. Incessant. Drove me crazy. His mischievous grin. Luke would smack his food (especially beef jerky) claiming that by aerating it, you could taste it so much better. It was obnoxious.

As a young man, he respectfully learned how to stand up to Greg. He challenged me when I needed it—attitudes, spoken words, thinking or talking negatively about a person. He only had good to say about others. He loved.

All the homeschooling days we had together from three years old to seventeen. Endless hours of reading together. Luke and Jace memorizing passages from the Bible as little boys. 25-page research papers in fifth and eighth grades. Spelling. Math. Luke building K'nex towers. Building a "power tower crane" that had 10,000 pieces, all by himself at nine years old. His creations. Magnetics. We were always teaching about You, Lord. Object lessons. Life lessons.

Luke waking me up at 3:35 am one morning. Him whispering, "Mom, can I talk to you?!!!" You had shown him what he was going to do with his life. He was so excited and burning with passion and vision.

Thank you for showing him he could talk and share with me, as he told me You had. That opened up hours and hours of honest, heart to heart, heart and soul communication. Challenging him, watching him grow, change, blossom.

Luke wearing suits for ORU presentations. Ethan, closest of friends and workout partner. Chris—lifetime best friend. Daniel—cousin and dear friend. His late-night poker games with friends. Motorhome trips. His RUNNING up the rock wall at Robber's Cave when rock climbing. He looked like Spiderman when he would shimmy up this one cliff in nine seconds. It took the average climber about five minutes. Crazy! Enchanted Rock, Colorado-climbing, hiking, and biking in the summers and snowboarding in the winters. Camping and hiking in Arkansas.

Lake Tenkiller. Him running out on tires strung with steel cable as a barrier and slicing his foot open within minutes of arriving. He had a one-inch circular scar on his foot from that. Forts in our woods, all over our 21 acres growing up. Chris shooting a rock with a .22 caliber and it ricocheting shrapnel back into Luke's eye. Miraculously, he had 20/20 vision in his eye after the surgeon removed the shrapnel. A couple of pieces worked their way out over the next couple years. Eye appointments. Dentist appointments. Luke not brushing his teeth for three weeks at a time while in braces, so he needed fillings in every single tooth after getting them off!!!

Taking a family missions trip together to Pine Ridge Indian Reservation. His deciding when we were there he was going to master the guitar. He realized the importance of music. He felt it literally could usher in light or darkness. He wanted to bring light.

Vail talk in the sauna the night before he died. Him wanting to talk to Lauren about her paper. "She killed cancer!!!" He was so proud of her! Laughing. His great sense of humor that he learned from his dad.

Ginger chews. Green/pink mints that melt in your mouth. Nori. Beef jerky.

Our trip to Mexico with our dear friends, the Guajardo's. Wearing Thing 1, Thing 2, all the way to Thing 6 shirts through the airport. Employees would laugh as they saw us and giggle, "You guys have a lot of things going on!" Surfing in Mexico. Late night swims in our condo pool together. Hanging out with the Guajardo's there. Beach walks. We climbed coconut trees to get the coconuts, spiked them open with the golf course markers, and "Twa-la!"—had ready-made coconut water bottles to walk along and drink—all eight of us!

King of the upside down green boat in our pond and the Tom Sawyer raft. Picking dewberries and blackberries together all over our property. The "family patch" named that because it was so massive, we could all pick there and fill our buckets.

I remember putting him and Jace on a plane from Tulsa to Houston to go to VBS at Baboo and Grand's church, Bethel. He was nine, Jace was seven. That was one of the hardest things I have ever done. I am usually calm, but I was a wreck. We decid-ed to drive down to bring them home because I could not stand the thought of them having to fly back home on an airplane without us. I packed all kinds of fun snacks, toys, games, and activities to entertain them on the plane. That was not fun for me.

He made deals with his siblings to get out of cleaning kitchens after meals. It cracked me up when his first job at Rib Crib had him in the kitchen cleaning dishes.

Homeschool Co-op classes. Playing baseball with Jacob Bradshaw. He always sat in the front of the boat. Doing 360's on the wakeboard behind the boat. I loved watching him figure it out, practicing the move over and over before he would do the trick. He was so incredibly good at it. With wakesurfing it was crazy when he would drop the rope and be back there surfing the wake without it, so close to us I could almost reach out and touch him from the back seat where we sat and hung our legs over the platform.

He decided to finish high school at Sapulpa and had to take an exam pass/fail on every class he had taken in High School. He passed every one of them. Every semester through college he started out downhill in classes and had to fight to make the grade at the end. He would never register for classes until the last possible day, every single semester! Drove me crazy! Before one semester at ORU, he showed me $3,000 cash of his hard-earned money, his part he had to pay at the start. He said, "That is a lot of money!" It was good for him to have that visual, he had skin in the game and knew he needed to make his school count.

Kettle corn events from fifteen years on. Him stirring the kettle. Him running events by himself when we had four going on simultaneously in one weekend. Ribfest. Mayfest. For years he ran the red tent down at the other end of Mayfest, while we ran the yellow. These past couple years setting it up without him has been so difficult for me. It made me so sad I just cried.

Hiring friends to run events. TU football games for the past eleven seasons. Jenks high school football games. Getting barbeque. Lots of laughs. Teasing his redhead cousin who showed up one day with his hair parted right down the middle, "Looks like the parting of the red sea..." Which was one of about eight puns that came one after another. It was hilarious, thankfully his humor was not usually at another's expense, but even his cousin was cracking up.

Throwing the Frisbee across the mountains, from one to another, at Enchanted Rock. Throwing it off the Colorado mountain and filming it. Awesome throw. We looked for it for what seemed like forever. The next day we had to go back and search again after he studied the video and was convinced he knew just where to find it. He did. Eventually.

Ultimate. Disc golf. Climbing countless mountains together as a family. Memory Lane. Praying together as a family.

Father, you gave him vivid dreams he would share with me. Often prophetic, warning dreams. He was always into numbers and what they represented. To him, 3-3-3 was a warning. He was very good at poker. On our cruise we took together as a family, two months before he died, they were advertising a poker tournament. The winners would play on successive cruises, which in itself was very exciting to him. He had a dream; in it, he looked at the cards he had been dealt. In the same hand, he glanced back at the same cards, and they had turned into 3-3-3. He knew then You were telling him he should not participate in the poker tournament. He expressed to me he realized that while poker itself may not be wrong, the environment in which it was usually played was. He knew You did not want him immersing himself in that scene since it often involved any number of temptations - alcohol, smoking, scantily clad women, even drugs. For the reason of his dream from You, he chose not to play.

He lived life. He struggled with addictions. He had a zest for living. I prayed for him for years. He had finally come into a relationship with You, after all the years of praying and believing for it. Planting seeds, watering the soil of his soul. Reading powerful Sonlight books to him in homeschooling. Thousands of hours' worth of reading. Teaching truths. Sowing wisdom. Sowing into his life.

Use him for Your glory in Heaven, Father. His warmth, his love, his heart, his embrace, his goodness.

At three years old Rob broke off Luke's front tooth in anger at Luke messing with him. Rob pushed his head down into a coffee table, and it chipped off Luke's tooth. I was dumbfounded that my three-year-old was capable of such a thing. Luke was always messing with his brothers growing up, provoking them, irritating them. Years later, Luke accidentally broke off Rob's tooth. Oh, the irony!

Luke and Jace's fight in the hallway. Jace was the same size as Luke since they were two and four. For years Greg would tell Jace he just needed to take Luke down once and he would quit messing with him. To my heart of mercy, this was appalling. Finally, one day Jace had enough. He towered over Luke in height by now. They got into it in the hallway, and Jace put Luke into a wrestling hold and wouldn't let go. Luke finally went limp. My husband was right. From then on, Luke did quit messing with Jace. He had a whole new level of healthy respect for Jace. Jace had finally conquered Luke, strong-arming him physically, after years of being challenged. It changed their relationship.

Luke, I know that you would like to ask Jace's forgiveness now. You wasted years that you could have been so close—you both being such amazing young men now. He forgives you. He loves you. He misses you. What made you always pick on your siblings?

Luke had just graduated from ORU and was waiting on You for direction in his life. The "how-to" to get the bigger picture. He had told Greg and I before graduating, "I just want to let y'all know, I am not buying into this 'graduate, go get a job right away thing'…" LOL. Fortunately, Greg and I were on board with that. We thought he would have the rest of his life (wrong on that one), to get a job and provide for a family. We agreed with letting him take time to do some things he wanted to do. What a blessing that was because we had him with us at breakfast and many dinners in the final two and a half months of his life here on earth. For that, we are eternally grateful.

Thank you for all the ways friends have reached out to us to help us cope with his loss. Friends of ours, Rob and Laura Koke pastor Shoreline Church in Austin, a congregation they started. They lost their 17-year-old son five years before Luke died. They put together a booklet with scriptures and some sayings at the end that so ministered to me. "God will so perfectly redeem this tragedy, and the beauty of His restoration will be infinitely greater than our suffering." I believe that.

Father, let me, let us, be a part of that. Give me ideas on how to reach others through the tragedy of losing Luke. "Satan meant this for evil, but You will use this for good, that many will be kept alive as they are this day." Genesis 50:20

Give me the words. The message. The strength. The boldness. Use this for Your glory. Use us for Kingdom purposes. Open the doors for us. I will walk through them with Your message of hope, healing, and life. Who do you want me to love, to speak, to invest in?

Writing all those pages in my journal of memories primed my mental pump. Ten days later I was flooded with more memories.
"Lived fully

Unconditional love, Uninhibited

Kissable, Yummy dimple

Easy going-smile, ways, humor (or Everything he did he excelled)

Luke loved Tommy. Tommy taught Luke to excel in bowling. He sowed into Luke's life and loved him right where he was. Luke bowled a 256. Wow. I am proud of myself if I break 100. He was at the center of fun, quick wit, and humor of the bantering between him, Jace, and Rob.

He did not like our dog Jonah. When we lived in Kansas, he was five, and the only child big enough to walk Jonah around the pond. So, he often did that, even though he did not love it. I guess that is why he was not wild about dogs.

I remember when we were out at Lake Keystone watching him, his brothers and his cousins digging holes in the sand to their waist. Later when we were there and the water was up, we would be wading out, and sink in these massive holes, the ones they had dug. I loved just hanging with him.

Him coming home smelling like Rib Crib. Funny how smells, or even the thought of smells can take you back.

Watching him grow in confidence and social skills. His depth. His sensitivity to the heart and feelings of others.

He was giving. His cousin later told me the story from the night he died. Luke, Caleb, and Jordan had gone to eat pizza, forgetting that Jordan's mom was making tacos for them that night. They had already taken up a table for the waitress. When they got the text about taco dinner and needed to leave, Caleb pulled out his billfold to give the waitress a few dollars for the inconvenience to her. All he had was a five-dollar bill, so he decided not to leave anything. About the same time, Luke pulled out a twenty and put it on the table for her. Caleb later told me he was touched by that.

On Luke's first week with a driver's license, he was pulling out from a Quick Trip. He hesitated, and a lady waved him out. He pulled out and hit another car. So that it would not affect his insurance, he opted to pay out the $7,000 in damages. We paid it for him, and he paid us back with money he made from working kettle corn events with us. He was so incredibly faithful to pay us back as quickly as possible. He lived broke so he could repay his debt. He would keep like 10% of his pay and give us the other 90%. I was so proud of you, Luke!

I love the man you became, and am thankful those are the memories we will carry with us. You will always be immortalized at twenty-two in our minds. I loved your embrace. The sweet way you would drawl, "Hey Ma-ma!"

I remember how you loved. You loved unconditionally. One time you were getting gas and an acquaintance/friend pulled up in his new car. You said to him, "Let's go for a ride!" You dropped what you were doing and went for a ride with him. He later remarked to his mother, "Who does that?!" You looked for the good in others. I love your soul and all that made you Luke. Like your daddy—you have a tender heart toward the Lord.

I remember when you were filled with the Holy Spirit at Dry Gulch years ago when you went with Luke and Caleb Koke, Remick and Jordan Lackey.

You were adventurous, like all of us. I remember us rock climbing when you were a baby and setting you on the ground in that backpack that would stand on its own. You would watch us and be content for hours. You kept that content heart.

I remember Cheesecake Factory dates you and I had. Top That Pizza date. Trips in the King's highway motorhome—our entry into "motorhoming" as a family. It was not more than a shell, LOL, there was no furniture, couch, or anything in the living area. We made some awesome memories in it though! Trips in the current motorhome.

All the years we went snow skiing together at Sipapu before you all were introduced to the more exciting slopes of Colorado. We went there as long as we could get away with it, LOL!

Once when we were racing (NOT literally, I would never race Luke since he could spin circles around me all the way down and still beat me) down the mountain, I came around a bend just as Luke made a jump through some trees, caught massive air, and then landed with a thud on the path ahead of me. He didn't move. Rob was passing over above us on the lift right at that moment and saw it happen as well. I screamed to him, "Get a medic!!" Luke passed out with a concussion. When he came to, he was extremely disoriented. He looked at me and said, "What happened?! I have no idea what just happened?!!!" That, by the way, was the first of thirty times he asked me that same question over the next twenty minutes. I responded, "We were racing down the mountain..." meaning he and I were booking it. He interrupted me and asked incredulously, "I was racing YOU?!!" That cracked me up, even though he was not in his right mind, he still had enough wits about him to realize what a joke that would have been.

Seeing who could set the record at Sipapu for beating the most cars on the lift. (If a person came down at an average speed and had ridden up on seat 14, they very likely would be on 14 the next ride up.) It was you—29 cars. You came down at that much faster of a pace, riding up on seat 89 and making it down and back on the lift for the next run on chair 60. Lightning speed. Hiking Vail mountain last summer. Hot tubbing at the condo. You and Rob biking down Vail Mountain.

You following Daddy down the street one Christmas morning as he played with your new remote car. The neighbor passing by, who snickered as he remarked, "Bought your boy a new toy, huh, did ya?"

Your daring, heart stopping jumps across cliffs when we were rock climbing at Robber's Cave. You tested your ability to the limit! Not to mention, my nerves.

Buying your first car, and later your motorcycle. You sold it to me after you had laid it down twice coming around corners and pulled your wrist. Oh, the irony. We purchased it back from you so you wouldn't get yourself killed on it. When I was an Organ Donor Coordinator we used to call them donor cycles, we saw so many deaths from them. You know the day we sold it? Daddy ran an ad for it when we were in Colorado with you. He set up an appointment for the guy to come to look at it the morning after we got home. We heard from the police at our door at 2:25 in the morning about your death, and the guy came at eight that same morning to buy your bike. Oh, Luke! I never saw it coming, Luke.

The Christmas morning you came down with jet black hair under a beanie. I never knew it till the gifts were over. It looked awful. Your daily grilled cheese sandwiches with turkey, goat cheese, muenster cheese dipped in raspberry chipotle. We

45

bought a food truck a year after you died, and sold your sandwich. We called it "the Lukester."

23 Mother's Day's

23 Father's Day's

23 Birthday's

23 Christmas's

Camping at Keystone Lake on your 9th birthday with about nine of your buddies—Daniel, Caleb, Beau, Chris, Jace, Rob, and several others. We blindfolded you, and several of them rode in the car with us as you tried to figure out what in the world we were doing. Spelling our names and taking pictures of it in the dark with smoking sticks that came out of the campfire. It was so cool because when we took the picture on slo-mo mode, you could see your entire name written out. It was mesmerizing. Entertained us for hours. S'mores over the campfire.

Poker parties up in your room. Jace says no one was as good as you. Hearing you play guitar. Your funny faces you made when you were playing and singing your heart out. Hearing you play through the air vents in the house.

You and Jace wearing Daddy's clothes as little boys, his warm-up suits, his boots. Putting underwear on your head with that silly grin.

Your talk with Toni and David when I got to be in on it. Your excitement and passion about the Lord. Your heart for Kyle. Your laying in our oversized green chair in the living room loving and cuddling Joy. Her exclamation every time you would walk in, "Lukie!!!"

Your buying iPhones to sell experience. Some con artist who sold you bogus iPhone look-alikes. Your clue something was really wrong and you were about to get taken should have been his asking you, "You are not a cop, are you? You bought four for $100 each. It could have been worse.

I love you. Father God, thank you for blessing our lives with Luke for twenty-three years (nine months in my tummy). You will always be in our hearts."

∽

Back row, left to right: Luke, Rob, Kim, Greg, Jace. Front row: Seth, Joy, Chad

I wrote this letter in my journal to Luke ten months after he went to be with the Lord:

"My time with you in 2015 was short. In so many ways, the last year of your life was your best year. Thank you for confiding your heart. It was when you pulled away in the previous years when you left for college that you bought into Satan's lies and pulled away from the Lord as well. Father, help me recognize these traits in any family member or anyone else.

You had become a man in your last year and a half. You were sensitive to the needs and hearts of others. You brought Jesus'

49

warmth and love into a room. You brought laughter into our lives and the lives of others with your quick wit and humor that was always uplifting.

You had learned the power of your words and never spoke negatively of anyone. You convicted me, even after you were gone. At the lake one day, I commented to dad about how sad it was that so many people in Oklahoma struggled with obesity. That day on the way home, a comment someone posted on your Facebook site popped up on my phone. He was talking about how you never said anything negative about anyone. Never. I was so convicted by you! I had just said that negative comment hours before. This was after you had been in heaven for six months!! You were correcting me, and you weren't even here! Someone this week wrote on Facebook about how you always made everyone feel like a million bucks.

Your life was cut short. Tragically short.

Sandy told me when you said to her, on your last night, you had decided you were going to get your Master's degree. You were going to take care of your dad. Wow! That is overwhelming love. That is so self-giving. You had NO interest in further schooling. What a commitment it took for you to finish ORU. And you did. You graduated.

You lived largely. You pushed your limits. My limits. Bringing me down that black bowl when we were skiing/snowboarding and later sincerely apologizing because it was way more than my level of ability. Too slick. Too steep.

You embraced adventure. You gave it your all.

You showed me we are all human with a touch of the divine.

Heaven is a better place with you in it. It is so much nearer and dearer to my heart with you there.

I always told you I looked forward to seeing how the Lord was going to use your talents and giftings. Wow! When I get there, I can't wait to see how He has used them!

I love you, Luke! You will always have my heart. Thank-you Father for my first-born son."

Luke–light; patron saint of doctors and artists

Gregory–watchful

We share many family memories of time out at the lake together. I can only remember one time ever that Luke was not at the lake with us. He loved it. He was a fixture in the front of the boat. After our first few times out together after he was gone, I asked Jace if it would ever be the same again without Luke. He said, "Never." From my journal months after he died:

"Father God,

My soul is crying out for missing Luke here at the lake with us. I feel so incomplete without him. I don't want this new norm!

Help me think like You through this. I am grieving the loss of him. I miss cuddling him in the boat. I miss his skinny body wake surfing; when he turned sideways, you couldn't even see him. He would never wear a life jacket to wake surf. We didn't even get to enjoy his bulked-up body that wasn't so skinny, (what should have been this past season) in the boat.

I miss his humor. His gentle ways. His gentle correction. I miss the strength he was. God, I miss him!!!

I always try to see him in Heaven with you and I know that is so good. I know he is bringing his peace, comfort, joy, and life. I miss him bantering with his brothers. It is not the same. What an incredible void.

∞

Rob was telling me recently about a breakthrough time he had at his week of Young Life camp as a leader. Facing fears. Fear of going off to ORU, fear of living life without Luke. Fear of his loss. Feeling like he has not been "Rob" since Luke died. He released those fears to You. The next worship song was about no longer being enslaved to fear but being free."

That is how our sweet Father God works. He is forever meeting us. Always at work in our hearts and lives. He is such a romantic, our Father God. He is always pursuing us, whether it is wooing us out of bed with a glorious sunrise to spend time alone with Him, or speaking to us in a worship song that confirms all He was just speaking and doing in us.

Rob's comments remind me of a comment Jace made later the same year. Easter was only weeks after Luke died. We took an Easter picture together of the family in bright Easter colors. Greg said this was our new norm. At Christmas, Greg wanted to use that picture for our Christmas picture to send out to friends. Jace said, "No, Dad, in that picture I'd forgotten how to smile." We all had.

Three days later, while still at the lake with the family, I jour-naled:

"We were in the boat—last run of our vacation with the fam-ily at Skiatook Lake. We were listening to Danny Gokey radio. A song comes on by Tim McGraw, "Live Like You're Dying." A guy (missed the story) decides to go skydiving, rocky mountain climbing…living with zest, which is how Luke lived every day. It was an overcast day. Greg starts crying. Jace, Rob, and I start crying. No one is saying a word, but we are all thinking the same thing. Sobbing. Hugging, holding each other. Fifteen minutes of sobbing. At one point, Chad comes from the front of the boat and says, "So, uh… what are we doing here?" Poignant. Pow-erful. Beautiful healing, cleansing moments. It honored Luke. It allowed us to mourn him—together. Makes us whole. The whole time we were in the boat, everyone was having thoughts of Luke. It was the perfect closure for that vacation.

The next day we joined the Mulready's (dear friends) at Grand Lake for a perfect day. On the way home, I texted Toni (my sis-ter) to ask if Jordan said "yes". (Toni's son Caleb was proposing to her that night on the beach in Florida). Blue moon—full moon. It was glorious. We watched a spectacular sunset over the lake on one side and the full blue moon rising on the other. Holy moments.

Meanwhile, Caleb was proposing on the beach in Luke's shirt, I had given to him, after Luke passed away. The one that was "SO" Caleb to me. The one he wanted to ask if he could have. It was very intentional, he later told me, that he proposed in Luke's shirt. He wanted Luke to be a part of the evening. He wanted Luke to be his best man.

Daniel (Caleb's brother) said, as he was walking up to Caleb afterward, he felt Luke walking with him. Smiling. Crying.

As soon as I texted Toni, asking whether Caleb had proposed yet and asked whether Jordan had responded—within the minute I got a group text back. "She said YES!" I thought it was Toni responding to my question. It was actually Caleb, sending it out from Florida.

I was thinking later, Luke would also have been Jace's best man. Chris's. Maybe Ethan's. Kyle's. Maybe Daniel's. Wow. They all saw him as their best friend. He would have been a grooms-man in Swan's wedding that had just taken place. Rob's wedding.

I sobbed last night realizing Caleb wore Luke's shirt to propose. Hearing Daniel's story. Thank You Father for letting him join us."

Daniel said to me sometime after Luke died, "I don't know if it is true or not, but I like to think the Lord allows Luke to be in on special moments he should have been here for." That has brought me comfort because I do believe he is now part of that "great cloud of witnesses" that are in on our special moments.

When Luke died, he was resuscitated and then taken by life flight to a hospital. We had the option, as a family, to donate his organs for transplant, which we chose to do. Some of the contents are redundant, but I want to share the letter I wrote to the recipients of his organs because it shares our story:

Luke's recipients' letter:

"To the recipients of my son Luke's organs:

I write this as we approach the two–year mark of when you received his life-giving organ. It may be months before you can read this. I myself was an ICU nurse, an ICU Transplant nurse, and an Organ Donor Coordinator. I had no idea when I was a young nurse, in my twenties, that one day I would make the decision whether to donate my own 22-year-old son's organs for transplant. I do believe the Lord had each one of you in mind then, knowing how strongly I believed in it and the many lives I saw impacted as a result of transplants. I worked on both sides of that. As a donor coordinator, I sat down with the families to tell them about their options in donating the organs of their loved one for transplant. I cried with them, grieved with them, and let them share about their loved one. I was often told that families found it was a way to make some sense out of their tragic loss. Before that, I worked with transplant recipients in the ICU, immediately after they received a transplant. I experienced the joys of them having a new lease on life with an organ that was doing what it was created to do in the first place. I formed relationships with these patients, some that lasted many years.

I have heard from three recipients that received organs from Luke - the beautiful woman that received his pancreas, the gentleman that received his heart, as well as from the wife of the man who now has his liver. All his organs were donated, as well as cornea, skin, bone, ligaments and tendons.

I want to share a huge lesson I have learned since losing Luke. I actually was very much learning this in my journey with the Lord for the year and a half before he was relocated to Heaven. A friend challenged me to start a list of 1,000 things I was grateful for, based on the book *One Thousand Gifts* by Ann Voskamp. This book has impacted my life more than any other book I have ever read, besides the Bible. At the time Luke died, I had written 500 things on my list over the previous year and a half. Since then, in the two years since he died, I am now at 3800 things for which I am thankful. It has given me a new lease on life. It has transformed my thinking. It enabled me, through the incredible pain of his loss, the grief, the struggle, to see the myriad of ways the Father has so richly blessed our lives. It allowed me to see and know His vast love for us in the most overwhelming ways.

Luke was the oldest of our six children. When he died, his two best friends were his 20 and 18-year-old brothers. In the times of sibling rivalry, in their growing up years, I always told them, "If you treat each other right, you will be each other's best friends for life." They became that for each other. We have five boys, and then, a girl. Every time Luke walked in the door, his sister Joy, who was seven when he died, would yell, "Luke!!!", and run into his arms. They would sit and cuddle in our over-sized chair for two.

Luke was a person that loved everyone. He would always find the guy off to himself at a party and draw him in and make him feel welcome. He had a smile that lit up a room. It lit up my life. He had this slow easy going way about him. He was a lover of adventure. In his words, "a boarder of everything." He would turn circles on a snowboard going down the ski slopes in front of me while carrying on a conversation. He longboarded, wake boarded, water skied, and he could throw a Frisbee to the moon. He excelled at everything he did. He had these crazy stilts, he would attach to his legs, that were two feet tall, and he could do a flip on them. He would go up and down stairs on stilts. I always told him he would be great in the circus. He could solve the Rubik's cube in a minute while jumping on a pogo stick! We have a video of him solving it in 5 ½ seconds. He loved playing guitar. His brothers and cousins, he played with, would laugh and say Luke was never afraid to hit the high notes. His best score in bowling was 256. He and his brothers would dominate in Ultimate Frisbee. He loved disc golf. He had his dad's sense of humor and was hilarious. Like his dad, he never used it at others expense, and I love that about him.

Luke had just graduated from college. The first two years he lived on campus, and then in an apartment, the final two he lived at home to save money on tuition to graduate debt free. He graduated with his younger brother Jace, who graduated early at 20. I had homeschooled them since kindergarten. Even at the time, we all felt like it was a gift, like we were buying back time, able to have them both live back at home with us their final two years of college. For that, I will always be grateful. Luke and Jace took every class they could, together, through college. They even got to work on their senior paper together. God is good. Luke loved Jesus passionately and had such a heart for others.

I wanted to share some about Luke since he is a part of you now. We miss him deeply. This morning I was sobbing missing him. Yet we have known deep joy even in our loss. We serve a good God, and we know we will be with him again one day. I pray God's blessing on each of your lives, and the lives of your families.

❧

I also want to include the letter we received from the woman who now has Luke's pancreas. After she sent it, I told my husband it was everything we would want to hear from a recipient, and that even if it was the only letter we got, it was worth it! She is a giving, loving, beautiful soul and her heart and life are such a blessing to our family. I treasure the thought of one day getting to meet her!

"Hello, my name is Cheryl. I am 49 years old, and I live in Indiana. I'm a wife, mother, daughter, sister, aunt, dog mom, and soon to be the grandmother of twins (a boy and a girl). Yay! I am so excited.

Twenty years ago, I was diagnosed with diabetes. I was devastated, as I was young, and had always been healthy. I couldn't imagine giving myself insulin injections. I learned though, and time went on. Over the years, little by little, the disease took a terrible toll on my body and health. My vision, my arteries, veins, heart, and nerves were all compromised. Five and a half years ago I was diagnosed with end-stage renal failure. I needed a kidney! Lucky for me, my then fiancé, now husband, was a match. He was healthy enough to donate one of his. It still took a long time, and two years of dialysis, before I was healthy enough to go through with the surgery. Two and a half years ago I got that kidney, and my life changed forever, back to the better. The only problem was, I still had diabetes, and it would eventually take its toll on my new kidney. I decided I would go through with another transplant, this time a pancreas, to rid myself of diabetes and prevent further damage to myself.

On March 24th, I got the call that there was a healthy pancreas available to me. It was a bittersweet moment. I was elated by the thought of no longer having diabetes, yet I was sad thinking about the person who had just lost their life. I couldn't help wondering about them. I may never know anything about the person who gave me the gift of life, but what I do know is this person lives on through me and the others who were the organ recipients.

I cannot begin to tell you how grateful I am for the blessing I have been given. Thank you for entrusting me with your loved one's legacy. I will FOREVER treasure this gift that has allowed my life to return to normal. I *promise I will take the best care of it that I possibly can. Thank you! Thank you! Thank you! God is good!*

CHERYL"

⦉⦊

I shared that because it truly has been gratifying to know that Luke is able to live on while he has enabled others to live. The organs the recipients receive dramatically changes their quality of life for the better. For a person to even go on the waiting list for an organ, they typically have only a year to live. It brings us great joy knowing that Luke made a difference for them. Luke was a giver. A giver of himself. Had he been given the choice to donate his own organs, I am convinced he would have.

Cheryl and I text regularly. She remembers us often. Though we have not yet even met, the relationship with her has been an incredible blessing. She recently sent this to me:

"Give my sight to the man who has never seen a sunrise, a baby's face, or love in the eyes of a woman. Give my heart to a person whose own heart has (known) nothing but endless days of pain. Give my blood to the teenager who was pulled from the wreckage of his car, so that he might live to see his grandchildren play. Give my kidneys to one who depends on a machine to exist from week to week. Take my bones, every muscle, every fiber, and nerve in my body and find a way to make a crippled child walk. If you must bury something, let it

be my faults, my weaknesses, and all prejudice against my fellow man. Give my sins to the devil. Give my soul to God. If, by chance, you wish to remember me, do it with a kind deed or word to someone who needs you. If you do all I have asked, I will live forever."

ROBERT N. TEST, #DONATELIFE

GRIEVING IS
NOT OPTIONAL

"I'm so sorry to hear of the passing of Luke Goodman. He was ALWAYS kind to me in high school. There was never a time I witnessed when Luke was anything but kind to others. He displayed the light of Christ in his love for others and his love for the adventures of life. If you knew Luke, you knew what it meant to see someone brighten at the sight of a friend while being the best friend he could be in return. I don't want to say rest in peace because that isn't really his style. Adventure on, Luke. Heaven will be your greatest one yet."

Rebekah Worrall McQuivey

"Time does not heal all wounds. It's what one does in that time that heals the wound. Sometimes it's easier to stay wounded than do the hard stuff to make things better."

- Sandy McKinney

The month after Luke graduated to Heaven, we had a kettle corn event. I struggled profoundly even to be there. As we pulled into the barn, I felt this deep, overwhelming sadness. It was dark, almost ten o'clock at night. I slipped out of the car without saying anything to the family, and walked in complete darkness, which suited my mood, down the rocky path from the barn to the house, and then the rocky slanted hill to our pond. I sat on our deck and cried. I sobbed for an hour and a half. I felt like my heart was ripping in two. I was missing Luke so severely. My heart was breaking. Then I began crying out to God, or maybe it was crying out at God. I was angry with Him over the death of my son. It was so unfair that he was gone at twenty-two. He had just lived the best year of his life, and now he was gone!

There is something that is so healing in tears. That night I cried until there were no more tears in me to cry and I railed at God. Then I quieted myself before the Lord and was just still before Him. I let Him meet me, minister to me, comfort me. Our God is so big. He is not threatened by our hurt and lashing out at Him. I certainly don't make a habit of speaking to him that way, but that night it was very much a part of my healing process. I stayed down at the pond, in the dark, after emptying my heart out until I felt the Lord's peace wash over me, mending my brokenness.

I was thankful to be able to cry my heart out in the solitude of our pond at night. The darkness matched the sadness of my heart. I was able to cry through to peace. I felt His love envelop me. As I bawled, the frogs became so loud, almost deafening, drowning out my sobbing. As I slowed to listen to them, their symphony became softer. I marveled at the wonder. The full moon was rising, reminding me yet again of His love for me. He loves us. He is for us. He has never been against us. I let His love wash over me like a healing balm.

There may be someone reading this that has never had a personal experience with the Lord. I have to be honest: I do not know how I would have made it through this experience of Luke taking his life without the Lord in my life. The Lord, the creator of the universe, wants to be in personal relationship with us. He wants us to know Him in such a real, intimate way. He says in the Word, the Bible, that the very hairs of our head are numbered. His thoughts toward us are as numberless as the sands on the seashore. Oh, He knows us. Every thought that crosses our brains He knows. He created each of us with a God-sized hole in our hearts so that we would desire fellowship and union with Him. I have known people that have said, "You don't know what I have done. He could never love me." The scripture says the only sin that cannot be forgiven is blasphemy against the Holy Spirit. Sin separates us from Him. If you have never asked Him into your heart, He is longing for you to do so. Ask Him now. He says, "Behold, I stand at the door and knock; if anyone hears and listens to and heeds My voice and opens the door, I will come in to him and will eat with him, and he (will eat) with Me." (Rev. 3:20) I John 1:9 says, "If we (freely) admit that we have sinned and confess our sins, He is faithful and just and will forgive our sins, and cleanse us from all unrighteousness."

There is no higher adventure in life than living life and walking out this journey with the Lord. He says His Holy Spirit will come and dwell within us when we invite Him in. He is my greatest source of strength. He is our comforter, our teacher, our help in time of need. No one is exempt from pain and loss. Every one of us will face it at some time in our lives and throughout our lives. I do not know what is ahead of me, but I do know that with Jesus, I can face it all. I know that regardless of what I come up against, I trust in my Heavenly Father. I know that He dearly loves me and that He dearly loves each of us.

Recovering from loss is such a process. It does not happen overnight. It is so different for every individual. Initially, my husband Greg and I found ourselves in such a "funk." Everything was such a fog. This lasted months for us both. I remember thinking, "How dare the rest of the world go on when I didn't know how in the world to keep on living." Typically, I am not a self-centered person. For the first year after losing Luke, all I could think about was him. I wanted to talk about him with others. I have many dear friends that let me talk and talk. They brought me such healing by allowing me to do that.

I wrote in my journal from a card I received a couple of months after Luke's death:

His absence is like the sky—spread all over everything.

This is a fragile time.

A time to be gentle with yourself

And to give your heart permission to grieve

To feel and to remember

Strength and hope will come again,

But for now,

Do what you need to honor this sorrow,

Letting your heart and spirit heal.

Grieving is not optional. It is a process and a journey. In *Nobody's Child Anymore*, Barbara Bartocci stated, "Grief denied is grief unhealed." Many are afraid to face the pain. They delay doing so by finding avenues to mask the pain of loss. Many turn to alcohol or drugs to drown the sorrow or numb the pain. Many allow themselves to become so busy and consumed with other things that they don't have to stop and face it. To become fully healed and whole after loss, we have to turn and embrace our loss, embrace the pain, and allow ourselves to walk through it.

> *Unless a person allows themselves to weep and to mourn, they cannot emerge whole physically, spiritually or mentally.*

When we choose to embrace it rather than run from it, it loses its power over us. It loses its hold or grip over us. The Word says that we grieve, but we are not without hope. Jesus wept over the loss of His dear friend Lazarus before he called for him to "Come forth." Other societies grieve the loss of their loved ones for an entire year. Grieving is not optional. Unless a person allows themselves to weep and to mourn, they cannot emerge whole physically, spiritually or mentally.

The grief/trauma counselor at our church gave my children a piece of paper that had a myriad of emotions people deal with after a loss. She asked them to identify feelings that they experienced through the loss of their brother. Most people deal with anger as one of the stages of grief. Guilt, remorse, feeling of abandonment, sorrow, helplessness, loneliness, feeling of disorganization, shock, depression, bitterness, hostility, resentment, even relief are all emotions people deal with as a result of losing a loved one. These do not just go away over time. You have to address, specifically, each emotion that you are holding onto. Pent-up emotions that are not dealt with will often later manifest themselves in the breakdown of your physical body.

I read a book called *Emotion Code* that teaches you how to identify, address and receive healing for all of these emotions. It teaches you to release them so that they lose their hold on you. Much of the disease process that happens in our bodies has its origin in pent-up emotions. You have to be intentional about letting go of these emotions so that they do not wreak havoc in your body. In a later chapter in this book, I go into in detail how you can experience healing in your emotions.

As Christians, we have incredible hope. I have learned to allow myself to focus on that hope. I can picture my son Luke in Heaven. I see him with his gorgeous smile. I see him loving others as he did so well here on earth. I know he is with others I have loved that have gone before. My precious sister Alli died when she was 21, and I was 23. Both my sister Toni and I miscarried two daughters. My dad passed away when I was 34. I have lost grandparents, great grandparents. I see him thriving there with all the rest of our loved ones. I know that one day I will be with him again for eternity. It makes the thought of

Heaven so much sweeter. He is with Jesus. That is where I want to be one day, and Luke is already with Him.

A very dear friend of mine lost her adult brother eight years ago. She turned to alcohol to numb the searing pain of her loss. Eight years later, she is still struggling. She admitted to me that she has never really dealt with her brother's death. She has helped me see how important it is to face and embrace our loss. She is one of my friends that have been such a help to me as she let me open up and talk about our pain. The pain never completely goes away, but it reminds us of the richness of the love we shared. We have to deal with it at some point if we want to get through it healthily. It has been over a year and a half since Luke died. I still think of him every day. It is no longer all-consuming, however. When I think of him now, many times, I can smile.

I have some friends that pastor a large church in Austin that lost their son. They knew they had to walk through their pain and loss to come through on the other side whole and healthy, and still be capable of pastoring their congregation. Greg and I decided we wanted to get with them, learn from them about their journey, what they have done to walk through their grief. They were a tremendous help to us as they shared their own experience, and what they have learned. There are many support groups out there that are amazing at helping with loss. It is comforting to find others that have walked through losing a loved one as well. With us, we have had such an immediate, incredible bond with other parents that have lost their children in death because of the pain we have had to experience.

When we were at Rob's high school graduation, just six weeks after Luke died, I remember my sister leaning over to her husband to ask about a woman who was there, "What has that woman been through that she has such a powerful presence about her?" Her son had died five years prior. Loss changes a person. It was evident that she had such depth in her character and her soul after her loss. She now has such quiet strength. I knew exactly what my sister was referring to. She had known unfathomable pain, but she did not allow it to make her bitter. She chose to grow from the process. It has shaped who she has become. It has brought out deep inner beauty.

In the book, *A Grace Disguised*, the author shares a similar experience. "I met a woman once whose presence made me weep before we even exchanged one word. She communicated profound depth, compassion, and grace to me. Something about her broke down my defenses. Later I found out why. She had lost two children at birth and an eleven-year-old daughter to cancer. She had suffered loss but had chosen nevertheless to embrace life. She became an extraordinary human being."

He goes on to say, "Catastrophic loss, by definition precludes recovery. It will transform us or destroy us, but it will never leave us the same. There is no going back to the past, only the future. Whatever that future is, it will, and must, include the pain of the past with it. Sorrow never entirely leaves the soul of those who have suffered a severe loss. But this depth of sorrow is the sign of a healthy soul."

Loss comes in so many forms. Losing a job, walking through a divorce, dashed hopes and dreams, and so many other things we face cause us to suffer loss. Rather than run from it, if we can turn to face it, and embrace it, we can heal. I have found that being transparent and allowing others to shoulder the pain with me has helped me get through. We all have to deal with stuff. Many try to hide the ugliness that is in their hearts and lives, but the more honest we are with both ourselves and others, and the more we allow ourselves to be vulnerable, then the more others can relate and even minister to us. As I have shared our story, so many others have come forward with their struggles.

As I mentioned before, there is a healing that only tears can bring. It is easier to cry in the beginning after tragic loss than it is later. I remember someone telling me, "Cry while the tears come easily." Initially, when the police came to our door to inform us of Luke's death, I had no tears. I couldn't cry. I was in complete shock. The tears came later. Greg and I cried together every day for almost the first full year. We would often hold one another and sob. He was such a comfort. When we would feel overcome with emotion, he would stand there and embrace me. We would cling to one another and cry. We both needed that, and we needed each other. An entire lifetime of raising Luke and all we poured into him was wrapped up in those tears. Crying is cleansing and brings healing. We are not always in a place or situation where we can shed tears. There were times when I would attempt to hold them back, but other times that I would just let them flow. When possible, don't hold back or repress the tears;

let yourself be okay with them. Tears are not a sign of weakness as we are often taught in our culture. They are necessary and essential.

On the 21st of March at 9:50 p.m., Luke pulled the trigger. The police knocked on our door at two in the morning on the 22nd to inform us. We flew to Colorado on the 23rd to be at his bedside as they declared him brain dead. At one in the morning on the 24th, they took him into surgery to be an organ donor. Every month of the first year after he died, those four dates were overwhelmingly difficult. Even if I was not aware of the dates until they were upon me, there was this deep, almost immobilizing sadness we all felt. After the one year mark, I have not even been aware of those dates at all on a month-to-month basis.

I had two friends that gave me the most overwhelming gifts I have ever been given - with the exception of my wedding ring. Amy had my house cleaned for me once a month for the entire first year. Trudy is a masseuse and gave me a massage every month for the first year. I scheduled both of them each month during those dates. They were such a mental lift for me at the time I was struggling the most. It was such a comfort to have my house cleaned. I have never in my life been less motivated to clean my house than in that year, and yet, it brought such peace when it was clean. The massages ministered to me on several levels. The health benefits were incredible and physically kept me going and feeling well. Emotionally, it was also so healing. Trudy let me talk and share where I was and what was going on in my heart and life. I came away from each session a little more whole. Her care and love saturated me.

I got together with two of my dear friends, Charla and Teresa, very regularly during that first year and did *Young Living* essential oil massages together. The health benefits are tremendous, but I cannot begin to place a value on how emotionally beneficial this was for me. We had hours to talk and process, and again, they let me share each stage of the journey. There is something about relaxing in massage that opens the soul and brings healing in such a powerful way. It was time that ministered to all three of us.

I have girlfriends that I would go to lunch with regularly, that would ask how I was doing. Sally, Michelle, Alisa, and Charissa just let me talk. It is so important to do just that. It was such a part of my healing process to be able to share my heart. Support groups meet this need for many after a loss, as they allow a person to share their grief with others who are also hurting. It helps somehow, to know you are not alone.

Many marriages do not survive losing a child. Both husband and wife grieve differently. I learned to give my husband lots of grace. It ministered to me to read all the cards friends and loved ones sent us for the first couple months. Greg did not even want to read them. He couldn't. He would be uncharacteristically gruff, short-tempered, and unloving. I had to learn not to internalize it, but to give him the space he needed and grace to process in his way. Not only was he dealing with the intense loss, but he was also struggling with finances and the added stress. He and I both learned not to have the same expectations of one another afterward. We were no longer the same. He gave me grace not to cook when I did not want to. I did not care at all about cleaning house. To us, lovemaking was an extreme comfort, to others, they are not able to for a season. There is no normal in grieving. The more we can understand that and not carry our usual expectations of one another, the more we allow each other to heal.

My friend that lost her son at seventeen made a room out of a long closet to memorialize him. It was a place she could go and surround herself with the things he loved. She filled it with all the things that reminded her of him. His basketball, his jersey, favorite shirts, hats, seashells, poster-sized pictures of him, pictures of him and the family and many other memorabilia. It ministered to her to go there. Her husband had not been able to bring himself to even go in there yet at five years after their loss. He gave us the privilege of going in to see this meaningful room before he had. He told us, "I will. I just haven't been able to yet." That showed me how very differently we all process grief and how critical it is to give one another the grace and space to do it in their way. He allowed her to make a sanctuary for herself to go to when she needed to feel closer to her son; she gave him the grace to not view it until he was fully ready.

Severe loss changes us. It is our choice whether we will let it transform us or destroy us. We will never, ever be the same person we were before, but we can allow it to grow us into a deeper, stronger person than we ever could have been before.

"When you pass through the waters, I will be with you; and through the rivers, they will not overwhelm you. When you walk through the fire, you will not be burned or scorched, nor will the flame kindle upon you." (Isaiah 43:2)

"Now may the Lord of peace Himself grant you His peace (the peace of His Kingdom) at all times and in all ways (under all circumstances and conditions, whatever comes). The Lord (be) with you all." (2 Thessalonians 3:16)

CHOOSING
THANKFULNESS

"Unless we make it a habit to give thanks,
we habitually give our family grief.

Unless we consistently speak praise,
we consistently speak poison.

Unless we are intentional about giving God the glory
throughout the day, our days unintentionally give way to
grumbling."

Ann Voskamp, *One Thousand Gifts*

My youngest three children, Chad, Seth, and Joy, were all born at home in my bedroom. Joy is our only daughter after five sons. A midwife delivered all three of them. Joy was both posterior and twisted as she was entering the world and it made for an incredibly painful delivery. The pain was ten times my previous five deliveries.

I deliver babies stoically. Greg and I took a Bradley birthing class in preparing for Luke's birth. In it, they teach a woman to relax with contractions (yeah, right) instead of becoming more tense. By the time Joy came along, I had long before committed to delivering my babies in this fashion. I was in such pain physically I wanted to let rip with some serious yelling. I was ready to throw in the towel and abandon any sense of control. But because I was this far into it, I continued intentionally relaxing with contractions, staying in control, and eventually, my precious Joy was born.

I made the decision to go with this method of birthing babies long before I was severely tested in having to relax through contractions as I did on my sixth and final birth. It was what I did. I intentionally relaxed with contractions regardless of the intensity of the pain. In the same manner, I was a year and a half into the process of learning to name gifts in my thankful journal when my faith was tested inconceivably more than ever before. I had already committed to this path of looking for the good in everything, of learning to thank the Lord in all things.

My journey in naming gifts and writing down 1,000 things I am thankful for has awakened me to search for the blessings in my life. It taught me to shift my focus. The Lord says to thank Him in everything. In ALL things give thanks. In everything? Even the loss of my son? I am thankful that he is with Jesus. I am thankful for the relationships He brought into our lives as a result of Luke's death. I am thankful for the rich friendships that have deepened because of the bond I share with others that have known loss. I am thankful that the Lord says He will never leave me, nor forsake me. He has walked every step of the blinding pain with us. He doesn't tell us to thank Him for everything, but rather, in all things give thanks. I don't thank Him for Luke's death, but I have learned to thank Him IN all things, even Luke's death.

I had already revamped my mindset over the previous year and a half by counting gifts. I had learned to hunt for His goodness. I wake up every morning, and in my devotional time with the Lord, I think about the previous day. I write three to twelve(ish) things I am grateful for in the day before. The day Luke died we were driving home from Vail. I was writing in my thankful journal how I was overwhelmed with His goodness. I was so grateful for our "friendship" relationships that had evolved, especially with our adult children. I was sharing with Greg how I was so thankful for where we were in our parenting; how very richly and deeply blessed we were.

I had a book study in my home with several girlfriends. Charla said in our discussion one day that she finds her deepest joy when she thanks Him for the most difficult things. I had begun this journey of a thankful heart, and I am so grateful that the Lord used it to prepare me before we lost Luke. As I previously mentioned, it took a year and a half for me to get to 550; three years later I am at 6200. If you think about that for a minute, do the math, if I continued counting gifts at the same rate, three years later I should be at an additional 1650, yet I am at 6200! I have to credit the Father, that shows His goodness to me in the most difficult time of my life. I have learned to turn to Jesus in pain and look for His goodness. My focus has been to be intentional about numbering these gifts. In the process, I have seen how deep, how vast, His love is for me. For each one of us. My friend Amy, that wrote the letter to the dispensary, said to me, "It is amazing that deep pain and deep joy can coexist." After Luke died, I didn't know if I could have joy again. A year and a half later, and even well before that, I do know deep joy.

I am thankful for Luke's 22 years here on earth with us. I am thankful for my sister Allison's 21 years. That is a pretty short dash for both of them. I want to share with you what I shared to eulogize Alli at her funeral. There were at least 700 people there. She touched a lot of lives. The week she died was a whirlwind. It felt like we were preparing for a wedding in a week with all the funeral preparations that had to come together. We often accidentally referred to it as "the wedding"–oops! What we were grieving on earth, they were celebrating her homecoming in Heaven. When our pastor came over to talk about the funeral details beforehand, he asked if any of us would like to speak at the funeral. We had not talked about it at all. My dad immediately piped up, "Kim will." That was my first thought about it. It was right; I nodded consent.

I never had a minute to think about what I would say until the night before. When I did still myself, I started sobbing over the loss of my sister. When I finally quieted, I said, "Jesus, what would you like me to say?" The entire eulogy came pouring out onto the paper as fast as I could write. I never changed one dot or one tittle. His anointing came over me:

"I am sure that if Allison, herself, were to get up to speak today, she would have opened with some joke and would have had us all laughing.

Yesterday as we went to pick out the spray for her casket, the woman was quoting the price for fifty roses. My dad asked what it would be for sixty-five roses and our whole family burst out laughing. When Allison was a child, she was unable to pronounce "cystic fibrosis." She referred to it as "six – five roses." We put sixty-five roses in the spray, so Alli got the last laugh after all. She had an incredible sense of humor and an ability, in the roughest of times, to always see the humor in things.

Allison was a rare breed. She was an inspiration to us all on how to face difficulties. Alli suffered much pain and hardship in her twenty-one years. She endured so much and had a lot of limitations because of her physical state, yet she never complained. She was a fighter, a soldier, a warrior, who had an indomitable spirit. She knew what it meant to love, to give of herself. Allison was a giver without ulterior motives, always desiring to give of herself, her talents and her creative abilities.

She became a professional clown, and her clowning abilities represented much of her philosophy of life. She desired to bring joy and happiness, light and life, to the lives of others. Through the years, many people have made comments about times when they came to see her or visited her in the hospital. She always cheered them up. In front of me is one of the cross-stitch pieces that she made. Each time she went into the hospital she put this above her bed. It read, "Enter with a happy heart."

She was always concerned for the welfare of others. On her deathbed, during one of our conversations, which took place in the middle of the night, while I was lying in bed with her, rubbing her back after a particularly painful episode, she verbalized to me that she knew she had very little time left. She told me about her concern regarding specific family members and friends, stating that she did not want them to become bitter towards God as a result of her death and that her desire was for them to know God. Dad reminded us yesterday of the scripture, "Greater love hath no man than this, than to lay down his life for his friends." In Allison's case, greater love hath no woman than this, than to live her life for her friends.

On behalf of my family, I wish to express our sincere gratitude for everything that you have all done. Our church, our family, and our friends have all stood by us so strongly during these times. Thank you all for your prayers, support, and love throughout the years. We would never have made it without all the strength you have provided us through all the walks of our lives.

People influence us in so many ways. Some people touch our lives so that we can never be the same. Allison was one of these people. Everyone who knew her expresses to us what a unique and special person she was. Our family does not pretend to have the answers to the "why's" of Alli's suffering and death. We had believed God to heal her, and we knew that He was capable of doing so. He chose a different path for her, and all that we can do is trust His Sovereign will. There was a purpose for her existence. Each of us here today can attest to that. Our family has become such a close unit as a result of Alli's life. We have had to pull together, hurt together and be joyful together. We are so thankful for the twenty-one years that the Lord saw fit to bless us with Allison!

I want to share a scripture that epitomizes Alli, from Philippians 1:20-21. "So now also Christ shall be magnified in my body, whether it be by life, or by death. For me to live is Christ, and to die is gain." I want to end with a quote from a close friend of the family. "Her life and her will to live, in order to help others, are beyond description by any words ever thought or spoken. She was unselfish and wanted everyone to see that God's way was the only way. To know her was to know God."

"We have confident and hopeful courage and are pleased rather to be away from home out of the body and be at home with the Lord." II Corinthians 5:8

I worked at a summer camp after my Sophomore year at ORU, Brookhill Ranch in Hot Springs, Arkansas. My sole purpose in working there was to be able to mentor under Hettie Lou Brooks that summer, a mighty woman of God. She frequently spoke on the radio, and I had great respect for her. After Alli died, Hettie Lou told me, "Alli was the most whole person I knew." The Lord did bring Alli to such a place of wholeness, as He did with my dad before he passed away.

To show how the Lord works, a very special friend of our entire family decided, as a gift to me, he wanted to have a woman put the eulogy in calligraphy. Alli loved making crafts for others, and she loved hearts. The woman that did the calligraphy wrote it out in four columns, without typeset in advance, to make sure it worked out on the page. It came out perfectly balanced. My friend Jeff framed it, unknowingly, in the same dark wood as all the furniture in Alli's room. The frame even had the same antique emblem as her furniture had. He included a picture of Alli with a heart on the sleeve, and the woman that did the calligraphy painted intercepting hearts all across the top; again, not knowing that Alli loved hearts. Really, she just loved. Hearts, to her, were an expression of love. The Lord's attention to the minutest details of our lives shows how deeply He loves us.

I did not intend to share the eulogy from Alli's funeral in this book. Last night the Lord laid it on my heart to do so; and again, this morning. My mom is currently walking through a most challenging cancer journey. This morning, as I include the eulogy, I get a text from a dear childhood friend, Lisa, saying, "I am praying for you, your mom and Toni." Here I am typing Alli's eulogy, that Jeff had done and framed for me, while Mom is having a biopsy done to determine if three nodules (that have appeared since her surgery last month are cancerous), and the Lord lays it on Lisa's heart, a state away, to pray for us. Lisa knew Jeff well, she has been there for me my entire life, was at Alli's funeral, has recently lost her mom and the Lord lays us on her heart to pray for us. He blows me away. The Lord is concerned about every detail of your life. He knows You intimately. He wants you to know that He is always there beside you, within you, walking you through.

Mom got the report back this morning; the three small tumors are cancerous. She will be going back into surgery next week, even though she had major surgery for this last month. Jesus used Lisa this morning, to show me how He has got us. She reached out, out of the blue, to tell me she was praying. I have learned through this journey how our prayers for others matter so much. They carry so much weight. Before we got the report, she was praying. I am so thankful for how He orchestrates the events of our lives. He cares. Not a sparrow falls that He does not see, how much more our Heavenly Father cares for us. We have to have the eyes to see. That let me know this morning, once again, how I can put my trust in Him. I trust Him with my mom.

Last week the Lord woke me up with my mom on my heart. Years ago, she wrote poetry. She thought in poetry. She has composed over 150 poems. They are beautiful, almost like prose, but rhyming. It was a gift from the Lord. I realized that in the richest season of her life, in her walk with the Lord, her poetry flowed. She has only written one poem over the last fifteen years. The Lord commissioned me to go to see her; help her think through and identify what it was in her life that shut her poetry down. Then, to pray with her and release His anointing over her to flow in poetry. Some of the poems she wrote were prophetic. He gave me a glimpse of her using this gift for eternity, of people in their mansions in Heaven having her poems framed and posted in their entryways. I did what the Lord asked of me.

Throughout her cancer journey, Mom has been an absolute rock, believing she would have no side effects with chemo, though she was on one of the worst kinds out there. Yesterday, when she got word of these three nodules looking cancerous, she cratered for the first time, even though she has been walking this for ten months so far. Mom cried and bawled and let it out before the Lord. Then she started writing a poem. It shows the angst she was dealing with, and she is not alone. I share her poem because it reveals the battle she has faced in her journey. Her surgeon even commented how she nailed the feelings and emotions so many other women have expressed as they struggled through a similar journey. This is her poem:

"Poured Out"

"Yes, this is the day the Lord hath made, but it's one
    I'd like to forget,
I really thought I was doing quite well; then the doctor
    had news I regret.
'The cancer is back; I'll get with the team. We'll decide
    on the way to proceed,
But surgery next week to remove cancer cells and a
    skin graft is something you'll need.'
After radical surgery just two months ago, this news
    was a crushing blow

Each time I feel like a hurdle is crossed, a new one appears from the foe.

I'm mad, I'm hurt, I'm ready to scream! This is just not
what I had expected.

His Word, His Truth, "I'm the healed of the Lord."

Is the report that I had accepted.

So great a prayer covering blessed my life that my
Faith in Him was great.

Truly it was a gift from God when the enemy tossed
me his bait.

I felt encased in a bubble at times; I thought the battle
was won.

But after today, I'm sorry to say, I think it's only begun!

The bubble has burst; I cried all day long, not knowing
just what to think.

My world's upside down once again, I feel like I'm going
to sink.

I've cried a bucket of tears today, all negative feelings
drained out.

Preparing me to hear from God, His perspective, while
giving up doubt.

I know God is faithful, though I don't understand. I'll
come through and trust Him again.

As I process the shock waves and give it to Him, this
battle together we'll win!

At the start of this arduous journey, the Lord gave me

a word to obey

I have not always followed through, but He's reminding me today.

"My child, take one day at a time and look for the good in all things

Trust not your feelings, only My Word and cherish the truth My Word brings."

The doctor's report was not good at all; I fell apart at the news

But God's report has never changed, so how could I possibly lose?

By Linda Swain

Like in my journey, the Lord told my mother to look for the good in everything. She has been intentional about choosing thankfulness. It has kept her eyes on His goodness and the way He meets her day by day. She has known joy in the journey. She has been exuberant at times. We have marveled at her. The Lord, in His wisdom, also told her to take one day at a time. Sometimes that is all we can handle. He knew she needed to keep her focus on Him; He has been her lifeline. Taking one day at a time keeps us living in the moment, not borrowing trouble from what could be tomorrow.

A week later, my mother wrote another poem.

"He is Enough"

"My Father, I am struggling today; so much going on
at the time

Surgeries, tests, appointments and such; confusion is
clouding my mind.

I need Your strength, Your peace, Your joy; my supply
is running low

But, You only promised each for the day from Your
unceasing flow.

I'm here now Lord to draw from You my portion for
the day

I'm standing on Your Word in trust You'll guide me all
the way.

You know just what I need today; You'll be my all in all

And as You hold onto my hand I trust I will not fall.

It's not an easy path I'm on; it's scary Lord to me

Some days I'm strong, yet others weak; so help me
Lord to see...

The lessons You are teaching me along this rocky road

To trust and rest in You alone, to know my hand You
hold.

A scripture comes to mind right now reminding me to
feed

On Jesus and His Word alone for that is all I need.

"My God shall make ALL grace ABOUND toward you
and me

And ALWAYS in ALL things we will have ALL suffi-
    ciency
That we may ABOUND to EVERY good work." And
    know it's not in vain
The trials that we suffer here are for eternal gain!
The seven all sufficient words remind me when the
    road is rough
And the feelings haven't quite caught up; still truly . . .
    He is enough!
(2 Corinthians 9:8)

By Linda Swain

Mom's poems were poems that related to the pain I knew in my journey in losing my son. My sister posted them on her Facebook wall and hundreds of others responded as they related in their own pain of loss. The principles the Lord was teaching my mom were the same He was teaching me. Instead of looking for all the bad and focusing on that, she and I both have l had to learn to look for the good. It has put us on a quest to hunt for the goodness of the Lord in our lives.

In my growing up years, in the week between Christmas and New Year's, Mom always encouraged us to set goals for the up-coming year. Not resolutions, as so many do, those are quickly broken and forgotten, but actually set goals. I have done that each year for decades. Some years I have been better about keeping them close in mind than others. This year, during that week, I took the time to look back at the goals I had set for the past year. I realized how few I met. My sister Toni shared that she and her large family have been coming up with one word to embody the upcoming year. How simple! One word. If we still ourselves before the Father and allow Him to drop one word into our hearts, He will give it to us. One word that will be the character trait we work on this year. One area that we want to see Him develop our weakness into strength. In our weakness, His strength is made perfect. I find that when we are willing and vulnerable enough to turn those weaknesses over to Him, He truly does perfect His strength in us. The area that was our greatest weakness can become our greatest strength.

The word He gave me for this year is "Joy." I laugh at the Lord's sense of humor—my oldest son took his own life less than three years ago, yet the word He has given me for this year is "Joy." We serve a Father that does not want us to be in bondage. He wants to free us to live full, whole, and healthy lives before Him. It is in His goodness that He wants to infuse me with His joy.

When we were growing up, my mom would put scriptures all over the house for us. On my bathroom mirror, she put, "Be ye kind one to another..." so that I would be more kind to my sisters. In whatever area we struggled, she would pray and ask the Lord for a verse for us. We were required to commit those verses to memory. She taught me to look for and lean on scripture to shape my character. "And the disciples were continually diffused (throughout their souls) with joy and the Holy Spirit." Acts 13:52. I want that! I want to be continually diffused throughout my soul with joy and the Holy Spirit.

I am about to embark, for the second time in my life, on a word study on 'Joy.' I like to take a word that He has laid on my heart, use *Strong's Concordance*, or a Bible app on my phone, and look up every single verse in the Bible that uses the word "Joy." I write out the verses that speak to me. I ask the Lord to show me His heart on this topic, to teach and train me as I study.

As I thought about joy, I realized how few people, even Christians, I see walking in it. They will know we are Christians by our love, and we should be a shining light to others. Overflowing with Joy. My precious niece-in-law told me this past year her word was 'Shine.' And she does! She shines for the Lord, even in some rough times I have seen her walk through. The word joy excites me. I have found my deepest joy in counting His gifts to me. He has awakened my soul to joy as I respond to Him in thankfulness and gratitude.

In Ann Voskamp's book, *One Thousand Gifts*, she says, "While I may not always feel joy, God asks me to give thanks in everything because He knows that the feeling of joy begins in the action of thanksgiving. True saints know that the place where all joy comes from is far deeper than that of feelings; joy comes from the place of the very presence of God. Joy is God and God is joy and joy doesn't negate all other emotions—joy transcends all other emotions."

She goes on to say, "How we behold determines if we hold

joy. Behold glory and be held by God. How we look determines how we live … If we live." I want to fully live this life here on earth. I want to thrive and be life-giving to those around me. It is up to us to choose to look for the good in things, to look for it in everything.

> "How we behold determines if we hold joy. Behold glory and be held by God. How we look determines how we live ... If we live." – Ann Voskamp, One Thousand Gifts

Isaiah 6:10b says, "That they might see with their eyes, hear with their ears, understand with their hearts, and turn again and be healed." He heals us as we see His goodness, and understand in our heart of hearts how much He truly loves us and pursues us.

My beautiful mom was sharing with me one day from a sermon she had heard about Caleb and Joshua in the Bible being sent to check out the Promised Land. They went out with a group of ten other men to spy out the land. They went into the "Land of milk and honey" and came back carrying a massive cluster of grapes between them that was so heavy it took two men to carry it. Joshua and Caleb came back with glowing reports. On the other hand, the ten men that went out with them came back saying, "We are as grasshoppers in their site." The men looked like giants to them. The put their focus on how intimidatingly large these people were, rather than on the promise the Lord had given them that they were to go in and seize the land. The Lord was displeased with the report they brought

93

back. Joshua and Caleb kept their focus on the good in the land and their mighty God who could deliver these giants into their hands. The Lord was pleased with Joshua and Caleb, and he blessed them for their uplifting report.

Choosing to give thanks is an intentional choice. I found that as I counted gifts, I have found joy again. One afternoon we were out in the hot tub about a month or so after Luke had gone to be with Jesus. I looked up at the cloud formation and exclaimed to the family that the clouds formed what looked like a massive hand. Minutes later the clouds seemed to configure the letters L U K E. It was an overwhelming, sacred moment. As we watched in awe, the cloud formation letters changed to L O V E. The "O" was in the shape of a heart. What a love gift from God! Tears streamed down our faces as we basked in His goodness. It makes me cry now to write about it.

Another crazy experience we had in the hot tub, which went into my thankful journal, was one night when Greg brought his phone out to the hot tub so we could play some music. He put on some worship instrumentals. We had previously heard an owl or two when we were in the hot tub. That night, as the worship song, "Holy is the Lord God Almighty" played, owls from all around us joined in, lifting up their voices in song. My eyes widened as I whispered to Greg, "Do you hear that?!" We both became silent, and tears began streaming down our faces as we listened with rapt attention. It was such a surreal, sacred moment. All of creation praises Him.

I remember my sister Toni telling me one day she was delighting in a cottonwood tree. It was as though it was clapping in delight with the gentle breeze. The Father whispered to her, "I have always loved that one!"

Luke's 23rd birthday was only three weeks after he passed away. On that day, there was this all-encompassing fog that enveloped us. It felt reverential, holy, like transcendent peace. My friend Carrie Kittinger, knowing it was Luke's birthday, texted me: "Praying the dense fog is a reminder of the dense cloud of the presence of the Lord in the Old Testament—His glory. May you feel the weight of His glory today." The Old Testament talks about the Shekinah glory—the glory of the Lord. That is what it was for us that day. We found Him in it, His Presence. That is so like our Heavenly Father to remind us in such a profound way that He was with us on that first birthday right after our son died.

One morning, months after Luke went to be with Jesus, there was a beautiful white dove looking in my bedroom window, right into my eyes. It arrested me, flooding my soul with peace and wonder. It reminded me of the white dove on the show "Touched by an Angel". It wasn't there long. It made a wide, graceful, glorious sweep around our back deck and flew away. Seth was looking through the living room window at the moment and came running into my room and exclaimed, "Mom! Did you see that white dove?!" The next morning it returned. Again, it looked right into my eyes. It was only there for a moment. It struck a chord deep within me. It was a gift from Him.

One of the flower arrangements we received the day after

Luke died was a gift from Vicki, a friend of my mom's and our family. It was this beautiful arrangement with white hydrangeas, soft pink roses, and white orchids. It was exquisite. It moved my soul. It reminded me of a bridal bouquet. I put it in the center of my kitchen ledge overlooking the family room. I felt peace every time I looked at it. The day I had to throw it out because it had died, my son Rob's sweet, thoughtful girlfriend Kellie brought me a similar arrangement. She had no idea how much I loved the first one, or how similar hers was to it. It had gorgeous big white hydrangeas, white roses, and white orchids. Again, it touched such a chord within me; it moved me.

Every time I see hydrangeas, they remind me of my dad. They were his favorite flower. He called them "snowballs." I was telling Joy how hydrangeas change color according to the soil. Alkaline soil produces a rich blue hydrangea; acidic soil turns them pink. Joy is all about pink. She loves pink. She exclaimed, "I would love to see a blue one!" Blue? Really? As much as she loved pink, I thought it was funny she wanted to see a blue one. The day I had to relinquish the second arrangement to the trash, I went to visit Sally, one of my closest friends. As I was walking up to her front door, I saw she had this gorgeous blue hydrangea plant. It was breathtaking. I pulled out my phone to take a picture to show Joy. She opened the door, and I told her how Joy wanted to see a blue one. She said, "That is yours. I bought that for you!" Wow! I was overwhelmed. As I was walking in the door with it when I got home, the thought hit me like a ton of bricks that the Lord was using the gifts of hydrangeas to show me that my daddy's heart was with me. When my heart was bleeding, the Lord allowed my dad to let me know how much he loved me. Dad had died nineteen years earlier. I knew in my heart that not only were the hydrangeas gifts from my dear friends—they were a gift from the Father, and from my father.

Amazingly, the story continues. An acquaintance, now friend, Dana, graciously offered me a day getaway at her cottage. She has probably twelve benches set around her property, all surrounded by beautiful vegetation and flowers. I sat in each one that day. It is the most peaceful, welcoming environment. It was a day that was all about Luke for me. It was three months before I was able to take her up on her offer, but when I did, she had cut an arrangement of soft pink hydrangeas for me inside the cottage. Dana told me she had never cut a hydrangea arrangement for anyone.

Before Luke died, I had never received hydrangeas in an arrangement. I had this heart connection in the knowing that both Jesus and my dad's heart were with me on that particular day. That day, I journaled everything I could think of about Luke. I filled thirty pages. I wrote it all—the good and the bad, while the memories were still fresh. I laughed; I sobbed. It was the most healing day for my soul. I spent the entire day embracing memories and allowing the Lord to bring healing to my heart. It was like I had primed the pump. Two weeks later I wrote another twenty pages of memories, all different than that day at Dana's cottage, of other memories about Luke that came to my mind. I will forever treasure those fifty pages of memories that flowed so fluently to look back on.

I encourage you to journal memories of your loved one while they are still fresh in your mind. Even if it has been several years since they have passed away, your memories are stronger now than they will be in a decade or two. It will be something you deeply treasure down the road.

On my birthday one year after Luke went to be with Jesus, we were working at Mayfest, our biggest kettle corn event of the year. My precious husband Greg went out before I woke up and brought back a delicious breakfast. Greg, Jace, Rob, Chad, Seth, and Joy all had the sweetest celebration for me as we ate. The kids bought me Chaco sandals and the Cepher, which I had wanted for quite some time. The Cepher includes both the Bible and the original 87 books that were a part of it before the early church edited out 21 books. I have read the Bible cover to cover numerous times in my life, and it has been a joy to read the Cepher. I was overwhelmed by my family's love and generosity.

During our celebration, I had such a sense of Luke's presence there with us. I felt him celebrating me as well. I had this poignant awareness of him. As we walked out to set up for the event that morning, Wayne, Michelle, and Hailey, that own the ice cream trailer two down from us, came up to me with a flower arrangement with hydrangeas as a gift for me for my birthday! They are from Wisconsin, we met them through Mayfest, and we see them once or twice a year at an event. It was so God! I started crying as the Lord spoke to my heart that He was using the hydrangeas to take this one step further, to make the connection for me that Luke's heart was with me as well. Each time I was given hydrangeas, it was so moving and meaningful. Each time was a gift, a caress from Jesus, from Heaven, from those that loved me sending me their love from another realm. The veil is so thin between heaven and earth. Michelle later told me she and Hailey both felt so drawn to that arrangement as they picked out flowers for me.

During this time Greg and I celebrated our twenty-fifth anniversary. He took me out to a nice restaurant in Tulsa, Waterfront Grill. While we were eating, our son Jace FaceTimed us to tell us he and his brother Rob were giving us a gift of a weekend away at a B&B in Hot Springs. When we finished our dinner, our waiter informed us our sons had already called and paid for our meal! We were overwhelmed by our amazing sons.

On that day, Jace posted on Facebook:

"25 years ago today these two incredible people decided to spend the rest of their lives together. They have faithfully loved each other since day one, teaching others to love by example along the way. Thank you, Mom and Dad, for holding on to each other through the good and the bad. Thank you for deciding that marriage is for life. I love you both so much. Happy Anniversary!"

We had the most delightful time at the B & B. It overlooked the water, so one morning we swam for exercise, and another morning took a canoe for a jaunt around the lake. We relaxed and enjoyed every moment together. Our room overlooked their gorgeous grounds. In the center was the most massive patch of hydrangeas I have ever seen. It had thousands of them in every color and shade. It was breathtaking. God is so good. He overwhelms us with His love when we have eyes to see.

I have to share my entries from my thankful journal that day:

2064 I am so grateful for the anniversary gift Jace and Rob gave us—that today we are going to Hot Springs, AR to a B & B for two glorious days together.

2065 I am thankful that six lives were saved as a result of Luke's gift of his organs

2066 For this glorious B & B Jace and Rob got for us in AR

2067 How You speak through the plants here in the beautiful garden, representing so much of our journey and the story of our lives together

2068 The Magnolia trees—early marriage—we actually bought our first house because of the Magnolia trees.

2069 Massive Crepe Myrtles—like I planted all over our property 15 years ago

2070 Rose of Sharon trees dripping with gorgeous color—I also planted these at our home. You are the Rose of Sharon.

2071 Bird feeder right out our window for my love of birds

2072 Even the room we are staying in is called the Birdsong Room! "Look at the birds of the field, they toil not, neither do they spin—yet even Solomon in all his glory is not clothed like one of these."

2073 Rosemary (tree), oregano, hostas, lilies—You are the Lily of the Valley, the Bright Morning Star- morning glories by the water, massive rose bushes

2074 For the honesty and reflection in our conversation on the drive here

2075 For Greg letting me see into his soul

2076 The canoe here—we get to explore while exercising and being out on the water.

2077 For the spectacular view out our bedroom window here

2078 The peaceful, beautiful waterfall that runs through the property here

2079 The massive hedge of azaleas—our love for them, we have had them in every house we have lived in.

2080 How the plants here seem to cover the range of the years of our marriage

2081 Hydrangeas in the welcome arrangement

2082 Calla lilies—like I carried in our wedding

2083 Massive butterfly bushes—I have tried several times unsuccessfully to grow them.

2084 The primo positioning of our room with a wide-open view of the lake. The rooms next to us have massive crepe myrtle trees obstructing their view.

2085 Being in Your Presence

2086 For the Wisdom You so freely give when we ask for it

2087 That Your mercies are new every morning

2088 Birds sharing bird seed with each other—beak to beak

2089 For the honor of loving Greg

2090 Breathing in Your goodness

2091 And Greg adds to that—for the plush carpet on the floor and our memorable experience here so as not to let our neighbors *know what we were up to….LOL*

*2092 Earl Grey tea Greg just brought me in my favorite color purple
mug for a souvenir.*

And here was a good one . . .

*2093 I am thankful that my journal just rode on the back ledge of
the bumper on the suburban for the past 100 miles and didn't
fly off or get ruined in the car wash!!!!*

Our time there could not have been a more soul-healing, restful, delightful time. It was an incredible gift from our sons and the Lord. It was what we needed to celebrate and nurture our marriage during a season in our lives when it was difficult to do so. We were so grateful for the generous gift from our precious, thoughtful sons. I was in awe of the Lord's attention to detail, how even all the plants in the fantastic garden represented the years of our marriage.

My ex-sister in law Melissa, whom our family dearly loves, gave us the gift of planting a live oak tree in Luke's honor. The Father cares so much about every minute detail in our lives. She had been inviting us for years, but we had never been to visit her at her ranch in Texas. We made our first trip there almost three months after Luke went to be with the Father. She had ordered this tree for him within the second week after he died, but for a variety of reasons the nursery had not been out to plant the tree for over two and a half months. The Lord's timing is incredible. We arrived in the evening and woke up the next day to soft rain falling. The men from the nursery showed up that day and planted the tree while we sat and watched from Melissa's luxurious, wrap-around porch. The rain was like Heaven's tears for us. We cried together watching them plant our tree.

Another experience that went into my thankful journal happened when our entire family was camping at Robber's Cave. We love to rock climb as a family, and they have some great rocks to climb there. Luke looked like a spider when he did timed climbs straight up a rock wall there. We had been there many times as a family over the years.

We made this trip after Luke had gone to be with the Lord. We had set up a climb we were all doing. All but Rob were paying attention when a guy looked over the top of the cliff down at us. We all did double-takes because he looked exactly like Luke. He was wearing the same Coca-Cola hat Luke always wore. He was wearing a muscle shirt just like one Luke owned. He was tan and muscular, built just like Luke. It was like Luke was looking down from Heaven to be a part of our climbing with us, since he so dearly loved it. He was on our minds that day anyway, as this was our first time climbing without him.

We all began exclaiming what a gift from God that was. Rob walked up, and we all excitedly began telling him what had just happened. He said, "I want to see that guy!" Just at that moment, for the second time, the guy looked over the cliff, right down at us, and made eye contact. God is so good. He cannot be outdone!

Another crazy experience that went into my thankful journal involved a day at the lake. Our family was out in our boat at Ski- atook Lake. We met up with some friends in the cove and tied our boats together. Earlier that morning we had seen a family at the pier with their twelve-year-old son that was ranked as one of the top wakeboarders in the world. They came in the cove, and invited us to join them for a ride to watch their famous son perform in their high-powered, very fancy, very expensive wakeboarding boat. Naturally, all the men/boys in our family made a mass exodus into their boat, leaving Joy and I in ours to keep an eye on things.

We waited and waited for them to come back. I never drive the boat—Greg always does—but Joy and I were quite bored by this time and decided to take the boat for a spin. Off we went into the main part of the lake, cruising around. It dawned on me about fifteen minutes later that I had forgotten to pull in the anchor. Oh, dang it! I felt so badly, and so dumb! I told Joy, "Well, the Lord made an ax float in the Bible for Elijah. We serve the same God. The Bible says, 'He is the same yesterday, today, and forever.' If he can make an ax float for Elijah, He can make an anchor float for us." We went back into the cove, and unfortunately, there were no floating anchors.

The next weekend our family went out to Keystone Lake. We were out in the middle of the lake, and I happened to spot a floating rope. I called Greg's attention to it. He pulled over to it and, you guessed it, on the other end it was attached to an anchor! Isn't that hilarious? The Lord was not limited to having me find an anchor in the same lake where I had lost one! This anchor was much nicer, bigger, and newer than the one we lost. He is so good! Not to mention, He has a great sense of humor!

2121 Full moon over the new upstairs deck with Greg and me sitting out together.

2122 Your provision for healing in plants.

2123 Best friend cousins.

2124 I am thankful to have had Mom for dinner tonight.

2130 Cloud window glimpses into Heaven's glory.

2131 Rain in July. Thunder rumbling.

2133 Feeding frenzy at the bird feeders on my deck.

2156 You got us off the lake early enough during the blowing tire ordeal and 2 ½ hour drive home from Skiatook. (Usually 45 min.)

2157 Chad and Seth setting up hammocks on the side of the freeway when we had our tire blowout.

2165 Time to go through Luke's room yesterday.

2166 Thank you for sleepless nights.

2173 Fondue around the dinner table for Joy's birthday.

2176 For meaningful talks with my sons about their girlfriend relationships.

2177 For fun together and enjoying one another.

2178 Freshly mowed grass, the smell, and the look.

2185 That light overcomes darkness.

2202 Greg being so capable of keeping everything running smoothly – boat impeller yesterday, torn belt replacement.

2206 Waking up at 6:15 am (by Jace) to be out on the smooth water by 6:30.

2207 *Watching my kids behind the boat.*

2208 *Jace and Rob both landing flips on a wakeboard and riding it out smoothly. Chad and Seth attempting backflips on a wakeboard, and Joy trying to turn circles on a kneeboard.*

2212 *Chad asking me, "Is there anything I can do to help?"*

2213 *Feeding my family healthy, nutritious meals amongst laughter and love.*

2218 *That You gave us the freedom to choose to love You.*

2236 *Yesterday was 20 years that we buried Daddy. I received a package in the mail, (only time ever), from Tim Maher, my deceased cousin Lauren's husband. It included the eulogies Toni and I wrote about Daddy. Father—what timing!!*

2240 *That Greg got to see 27 shooting stars with the meteor shower the other night.*

2248 *Thank you that there was good motivation, Jace moving home, to have to clean out Luke's room.*

2249 *Mist rising on the pond.*

2266 *For sunlight on dew sparkling.*

2268 *Leaves swaying and singing Your praise.*

2278 *You there for me when I crater like I did yesterday.*

2283 *Joy changing from outfit to outfit to dance with her new DVD today. I would love to have had an hour to sit and watch her. I saw her in four outfits, ballet bun. I love her so.*

2284 *That through losing Luke, I learned, for the first time in my life, how much you really love me. Your love is so vast, so far-reaching, so deep, so good. I love you, Father.*

2285 *I am thankful that You are near to the brokenhearted.*

2286 *I am thankful that my mother taught me to place such im-*
portance on sitting down to dinner together as a family. In
this crazy-paced world that is so rare these days. It has been
like glue for us.

In *Tracks of a Fellow Struggler*, John Claypool said, "The way
of gratitude does not alleviate pain, but it somehow puts some
light around the darkness and creates strength to begin to move
on."

Colossians 3:15, "And let the peace (soul harmony which
comes) from the Christ rule (act as umpire continually) in your
hearts – deciding with finality all questions that arise in your
minds – (in that peaceful state) to which as members of Christ's
one body you were also called to live. And be thankful – appre-
ciative, giving praise to God always."

And from my journal from *Jesus Calling*, "Learn to enjoy life
more. Relax, remembering that I am God with you. I crafted
you with an enormous capacity to know Me and enjoy My presence. When my people wear sour faces and walk through their
lives with resigned rigidity, I am displeased. When you walk
through a day with childlike delight, savoring every blessing,
you proclaim your trust in Me, your ever-present shepherd. The
more you focus on My presence with you, the more fully you
can enjoy life. Glorify Me through your pleasure in Me. Thus,
you proclaim my presence to the watching world."

My mother-in-law passed away recently after a decade of battling Alzheimer's disease. She was a gift to me; I could not have dreamed of a more perfect one. In her right mind, she was gracious, loving, warm, welcoming, hospitable, and caring. She never "over-stepped" as mothers-in-law are often known to do. Years ago, I cried to my husband feeling like I had already lost one of my dearest friends because when my son died, she was too far gone in her memory to even tell her of his death. She would have relived it seconds after hearing of it, as though she had just heard it for the first time.

Months before she passed away, we planned a trip with my father-in-law to take him at 96 years old to Galveston, where he was born. My son Rob was going to be in-between a month-long summer missions trip to Zimbabwe and a month-long marketing trip through school to Brazil. We planned this trip to take place during the small window of opportunity when we had him home for the summer, so that he could join us.

At the time of the trip, my mother-in-law had declined to the state where she had not eaten in the past seven days, and we knew that the end was near for her. The entire family was with us. I leaned down and whispered in her ear, "I love you, Natalie. You will be with Jesus soon. Please give Luke my love for me." She looked into my eyes, and said the only thing with clarity that she was able to say to any of us: "That was a nice talk." What a gift! It was a kiss to me from the Father to receive that response from her. Like a hug from Heaven, as one woman expressed to me.

I marveled how in this final week of her life every one of her children and grandchildren were able to be at her bedside. One grandson even came from Russia to say goodbye. The Lord cares so intimately about the details of our lives that He orchestrated all of us having the opportunity to see her this one last time before she went to Heaven.

In Kat Kerr's teachings, she tells the story of how when a loved one dies, they are escorted to Heaven by saints that have gone before. She said that there are times when Jesus himself will come to take someone home. She witnessed Oral Roberts being picked up in a chariot by Jesus. While we were in Galveston with the rest of the family, my sister-in-law Gail was at Natalie's bedside. Natalie looked toward the window and said the only other coherent words she had before she went into a coma and died. "There are people over there." Gail looked and saw no one. She asked, "Who do you see?" Natalie responded, "I see Moses." What?! Was Moses was coming to escort her to her heavenly home? We stood in awe, not just of the fact that Moses was escorting her to Heaven, but that she was able to communicate that to us.

It is in choosing thankfulness that He opens our eyes to see the myriad of ways that He communicates, "I love you." 1,000 gifts—they are all gifts from the Father to us. They are all the ways He is continually blessing our lives. Like my friends Rob and Laura Koke wrote in a pamphlet they sent us after they lost their son Caleb, "The Father uses all the resources of Heaven to minister to us in our time of grief." It is in this counting of gifts, in recognizing all the resources He uses to minister to us, that He has lifted me from pain to deep-seated Joy. I plan to be at 10,000 in my thankfulness journal one day, even 20,000. Actually, at the end of my journey here on earth, I would like to be at 100,000. It is a habit that I intend to keep for a lifetime.

NAVIGATING THROUGH GRIEF

"Today marks six months since the loss of my oldest brother. Luke, you are so incredibly missed. Not a day goes by without me thinking about you and relishing the amazing memories we share. You're a real hard one to lose, and your absence from this world has left myself and so many others with a painfully large hole in our lives. I can only rest in the peace the Lord instills. For I know that you're sitting in His presence, waiting for us to come home soon. I love you dearly brother, and I can't wait for the day I get to whoop your butt on the heavenly disc golf courses!"

Rob Goodman

As I mentioned in the letter to the recipients of Luke's organs, as my boys were growing up and going through the sibling rivalry that marks so many homes, I would often tell them, "If you treat each other right, when you grow up you will be each other's best friends for life." My boys, now young men, have become that. They did learn to treat one another right. Luke was 22 when he graduated to Heaven. Rob had just turned 18. Luke, Jace, and Rob all shared similar interests that we cultivated as a family. We have been on numerous camping trips together. We hike, rock climb, bike ride, play disc golf, throw Frisbees, snow ski and board, and spend countless hours in the summer in the boat together. All five of our boys, Chad and Seth included, can do crazy stunts behind the boat. Luke, Jace, and Rob all have different tricks they do on wakeboards like tangents, 360's, and various other bodily contortions. I love watching them all.

I have loved watching their friendships emerge. They would just as soon hang out with one another as with anyone else. They love and cherish being together. They have become each other's best friends. They would all play Ultimate Frisbee together, play volleyball with friends, weight-lift together, take rafting trips with each other. I would love when Luke would include Rob to go hang out with his friends. Jace, 21, and Rob, 18, included Chad, 14, on a ski trip with college buds last winter, and are doing so again this year. It is a joy seeing them grow up and love one another.

Rob went off to college six months after he lost his brother. He was in a completely new and different environment. Toward the end of his school year he commented to me, "Mom, there are only two guys on my entire floor that even know that I lost my brother this year." Wow. After Luke's death, none of his peers that knew Luke even mentioned his loss. The two people in his life that were a support during that time were his girlfriend Kellie and his friend John Daugherty. John had lost his dad two years earlier. He had reached out to Rob through youth group and had taken him under his wing. He was incredible for Rob and our family. He would randomly show up with meals for our entire large family to let us know he was thinking of us. He would bring us bagels. He allowed Rob to open up and talk about his journey.

I was 23 when my younger sister died. She had cystic fibrosis and scoliosis, with a 102-degree curvature of her spine. Her life and death brought our family closer together, and brought us much closer in our walks with the Lord. She had Harrington rods inserted in her spine, and while she was in the hospital recuperating, she developed a nosocomial (hospital-acquired) infection of Legionnaires' disease from the hospital air vents. It took her life, as she was immunosuppressed from the cystic fibrosis.

I had been involved in leading a mission's trip in Guatemala, and when I came home I went straight to her bedside in the hospital. She rallied when I arrived, and I was there with her for the next seventeen days. I had been off at college for the previous four years, and I stayed home with my parents after her death. My dad had a restoration company and took a job in Waxahachie, TX, hours away from our home in Houston. I was working at St. Luke's Hospital as a transplant ICU nurse and had a 45-minute commute. I had no support system after losing my sister. I had been gone for four years, and all my friends had moved on. The Lord sent me one precious friend, Jane, who was 44, twice my age. She was agnostic and did not believe in God. Ironically, He used her to minister to me when she befriended me during that time. She was God's gift to me, whether she believed in Him or not. I had no idea what to do with my grief—I just suppressed it. Probably, as a result, I was in seven car wrecks over the next year-and-a-half. Suppressed grief can be very destructive. My friend Jane allowed me to explore my grief, and she was a Godsend.

Rebecca Wagner Systema says in an article I recently read, "It is important for us to not deny our pain, and to take time to mouth our losses. Without giving ourselves time to grieve, our wounds may never heal." When Luke died, I realized from losing my sister how important it was for our family to be a support system for one another. I am an avid reader, when I have the time. When we went to Austin to visit my friends Rob and Laura, as they too had lost their son, they told Greg and me that they read everything about loss and grief they could get their hands on after their son Caleb went to be with Jesus. At that time, I was frequently sharing things with my family that I would read about dealing with and walking through loss. It opened the way for many meaningful conversations that we all needed to have. They allowed us to be able to talk about what we were going through.

With my younger children, Chad, Seth, and Joy, I often verbalized feelings related to our loss, since they were not old enough to do so themselves. Our grief counselor at church said,

"Your younger ones are not going to have the tools to deal with loss yet that your older ones have." Joy adored Luke. After his death, she almost never talked about him. Those feelings need to be aired. At times, when I see her overreacting emotionally in a situation, I am aware that it is related to her grief. I verbalize that for her, and she often begins sobbing and just cuddles with me.

Years ago, I read an email. It said, "So, you have just gotten married, congratulations! Now, get yourself some girlfriends!" It went on to explain that when we marry, many of us expect our husbands to be our lifelong confidante. He can be that, but that there is a need that girlfriends meet on an emotional level that our husbands may not. My girlfriends have been critical to my healing process. I had friends from every stage of my life that we there for me when Luke died. They flew in from all over the country. If they could be there, they were. I don't know what I would have done without them. They would call regularly from around the country to check up on me or text to let me know they were praying for me. I have the best girlfriends in the world, and my sister and mom are two of them. My mother is my prayer warrior. She takes every need we have to her prayer group and church, and they cover us in prayer. My sister is my lifelong confidante; I can share anything with her and seek out her wise counsel. Surrounding yourself with good, healthy relationships, where you allow yourself to be vulnerable and real with other individuals, is one of the healthiest ways to journey through all of life—the good times and bad. It is never too late to make new friends.

I was shocked at the lack of support for my son Rob among his friends. At his age, very few of his friends have known significant loss. Many people have no idea what to say to someone who has lost a loved one. It is not that they don't care, they just do not know how to address the pain and loss. Many people, family and friends included, don't bring up a person's loss because they think, "If they are doing fine right now, I don't want to make them cry." So what if you do? Crying is good. Crying is healing. Mention their loved one's name. They need to know you have not forgotten. They need to know you care. It is amazing to me how few people ever even say Luke's name to me since he died. It is ok, it is more than ok, to do so. His name was a household name for us before; it is certainly ok to talk about him now. I have known other parents that have lost a child, other friends that have lost a spouse, a parent, or a loved one, and they all lament to me over the same thing. Never be afraid to mention their loss. You may be one of the only ones who do. If they want to talk, let them. Give them room. Ask leading questions. I am grateful even now when friends text me to say I have been on their minds, and ask how I am doing.

I am big on journaling. Years ago, when I was in high school, I went on a retreat. Rachel Cook Burchfield was the speaker and woman running the retreat. She was a mentor to me and my "spiritual mom." She had all of us find a spot in the woods to be alone with the Lord and pour out our hearts in our journal. Then she directed us to still ourselves and our hearts before the Lord, wait upon Him, and then journal what we think He would respond to us. I found that as I did this, I would hear from Him. I would receive from Him. I would start writing, and the answer from Him would pour out on my pages. This method was how I learned to listen to His voice. I still do it today, years later. It is one of the ways I hear from Him most effectively because as I write, I am not distracted and allowing my mind to wander.

He asks us to "Be still and know that I am God." Ps. 46:10. (KJV) I find that in the crazy business of my days, I can stop for two–three minutes at a time, two–three times a day and still myself before Him. I can enter His presence, and know that He is God. It grounds me, centers me, and reminds me to keep Him as my focus. One of the scriptures that has ministered to me the most through Luke's death is: "You will keep him in perfect peace whose mind is stayed on You, because he trusts in you." (Isaiah 26:3, ESV) I do find peace that only the Lord can give as I trust Him in everything. I trust Him with my life. The other verse that has ministered so much to me in this time has been Romans 15:13: "May the God of hope fill you with all joy and peace as you trust in Him, so that you may overflow with hope through the power of the Holy Spirit." (NIV)

> "May the God of hope fill you with all joy and peace as you trust in Him, so that you may overflow with hope through the power of the Holy Spirit." (NIV)

I am reminded of some of my dad's final words before he went to be with the Lord. He died of esophageal cancer. He was in a coma for many of his last days here on earth. He awoke at one point, looked around the room completely lucid and said, "It is so good to be able to trust in Him." Then he slipped back into his coma. What a gift that was to us, to know my dad was in a place of total trust and comfort, and in the Father's arms.

One of the most significant ways I have found comfort in journeying through grief has been through my devotions with the Lord every morning. I found I could have no less than an hour with Him every morning to receive the manna I needed to get through the day. His mercies are new every morning. I often was stair-stepping on a machine in my bedroom while reading His word and every book I could get my hands on about grieving. I would find the next book through the quotes I would gather in the book I was reading. I read book after book and discovered so much help in walking through the grieving process.

One little set of books that ministered to me the most is a four-part series entitled *Journeying Through Grief* by Kenneth Haugk. The author wrote it in a style that gives you bite-size nuggets to deal with as you are walking out the grieving process. It is tremendous. It is designed for a person to read book one three weeks after their loss, the second book three months after, the third six months after, and the final book eleven months after. I give them to others that have known the loss of a loved one, probably twenty sets by now. They ministered immensely to me.

On the day Luke died, we were driving home from Colorado, and as we were going through city after city and switching radio stations, we heard the Chris Tomlin song, "Jesus Loves Me, He is For Me" three, if not four times on the way. My brother-in-law

David has always said, "Jesus loves you, He is for you, and He has never been against you." I looked at Greg and commented how it was amazing that we heard it so many times on the way home. It was like the Lord used the song to prepare us for what was about to happen in our lives. When the police came to our door that night to tell us about our son, that song kept running through my mind. *Jesus loves you. He is for you. Jesus loves you. He is for you.* It was my strength.

In the midst of the most horrific tragedy I could ever imagine, Jesus loved me, and He was for me, was absolutely what carried me the first couple of days. The enemy comes to steal, to kill, and to destroy. The Father wants us to know that He is a good God that loves us, and we can completely put our trust in Him to walk through anything.

I have also found so many verses that have ministered to me through this season of my life. A couple of weeks after Luke died, we were in Austin visiting Greg's parents. We had dinner with them, his sister, and my niece and nephew. As we were leaving the restaurant, my niece piped up to say that Joy could ride back to the retirement village with her. I had this instantaneous, panicky reaction—I couldn't let my seven-year-old daughter ride separately from me at that time. I am not an anxious person, and that was a response I had because I had just lost my son. I caught myself and made an intentional decision that I was not going to walk or live in fear. Psalm 112:7 says, "He shall not be afraid of evil tidings; his heart is firmly fixed, trusting (leaning on and being confident in) the Lord." I had to decide consciously to trust my daughter Joy with the Lord. I was not going to walk in fear. I allowed her to ride with my niece, and I was at peace within myself. I do have to say, it was quite a relief when they showed up there soon after we did.

Isaiah 41:10 says, "Fear not: for I am with you; do not look around you in terror and be dismayed for I am your God. I will strengthen you and harden you to difficulties, yes, I will help you; yes, I will hold you up and retain you with My victorious right hand of rightness and justice."

Psalms 147:3, "He heals the brokenhearted and binds up their wounds (curing their pains and their sorrows)."

Psalms 34:18, "The Lord is close to those who are of a broken heart, and saves such as are crushed with sorrow for sin and are humbly and thoroughly penitent."

Hebrews 13: 5b–6, "God has said, 'Never will I leave you; never will I forsake you.' So, we say with confidence 'The Lord is my helper; I will not be afraid.'" (NIV)

2 Corinthians 12:9-10, "My grace – My favor and loving-kindness and mercy – is enough for you (sufficient against any danger and to enable you to bear the trouble manfully); for My strength and power are made perfect and show themselves most effective in your weakness. (It seems that is all I have to offer these days…) Therefore, I will all the more gladly glory in my weaknesses and infirmities, that the strength and power of Christ, the Messiah, may rest – yes, may pitch a tent over and dwell upon me. So, for the sake of Christ, I am well pleased and take pleasure in the infirmities, insults, hardships, persecu-

tions, perplexities, and distresses; for when I am weak (in human strength) then I am truly strong – able, powerful in divine strength."

Psalms 62: 5–8, "My soul, wait only upon God and silently submit to Him; for my hope and expectation are from Him. He only is my rock and my salvation; He is my Defense and my Fortress; I shall not be moved. With God rests my salvation and my glory; my Rock of unyielding strength and impenetrable hardness, and my refuge is in God. Trust, lean on, rely on and have confidence in Him at all times, pour out your heart before Him, God is a refuge for us (a fortress and a high tower)."

Exercise is another area that can help you navigate through grief. I mentioned stair-stepping earlier. Exercise has always been a consistent part of my life. I have found it not only keeps me physically healthy, but healthy emotionally as well. Our family is extremely active, and we love doing athletic things together, whether that be pickleball, tennis, hiking, biking, water sports, swimming across the lake together, rollerblading, volleyball, walking, ping-pong, or whatever else. Exercise releases endorphins, which give us a mental lift and helps us feel better about ourselves and our world. It strengthens and equips us, and is a great outlet for releasing pent up emotions related to grief. It is a healthy alternative to other ways of dealing with loss that keeps you physically and emotionally strong. It helps you feel better about yourself in a time when a healthy self- image is important to your well-being.

We all grieve differently. We have to have a lot of grace with one another when we are grieving, especially within a family where all our worlds have been rocked by loss. There were times, especially in the first year, when my husband would be short and ill-tempered with me for no apparent reason. I learned to recognize he was lashing out because of his pain and not to take offense. Through loss, the huge thing is to communicate. My mom taught me the importance of timing—waiting for the right opportunity or moment to address sources of conflict. It may not be right timing in the heat of the moment, but I have learned to come back to it at a later time, when the situation has defused, to talk through an issue. That way tempers do not flare, and both sides can resolve things without angst.

When I was growing up, Mom would never let us run to Dad, as he was walking in the door after a long, stressful day at work, and say, "The dishwasher is broken!" or anything else he did not want to hear right then. We learned to welcome him home, and let home be a haven for him. Mom would take an afternoon nap to make sure she was rested and cheerful, then freshen her makeup, put on soft music or worship music, light candles, and have dinner cooking in the oven with delicious smells wafting through the air as he walked in the door. No, she didn't vacuum in pearls like on "Leave it to Beaver." But she did learn, and taught us, to set an atmosphere in the home that was warm, inviting, and welcoming.

Later, when he was in a relaxed frame of mind, we could

bring up the broken dishwasher or whatever else. He would be ready to receive it and able to handle it. It is the same way when walking through grief. I have learned to delay controversy; it is okay to do so until both parties are in a relaxed frame of mind and can deal with it healthily. My husband, Greg, and I have what we call "couch time" when he gets home in the evenings. I try to stop what I am doing and sit with him on the couch to hear about his day. It lets him know he is valued and loved.

Losing a child is a significant stress on a marriage. It is so important to nurture a relationship after a loss like that. There may be things that need to be forgiven in light of it. Both husband and wife may need to choose forgiveness and not place blame on one another. It is also important to forgive yourself. If needed, ask for forgiveness from your spouse, as well as from your Heavenly Father, and others you have offended. Greg and I have been an enormous support to each other while grieving the loss of our son. We have needed one another. After twenty-eight years of marriage, we still go on regular dates together. We make our dates a time for fun and enjoyment. They are not the time to bring up issues with the kids or other concerns. There are times concerns need to be addressed, but we like to keep our dates as times that we love being together.

Talk with others that are also deeply affected by the loss. Transparency is so freeing. Choose not to hide the process. Let others lend you strength when you don't have it. Every time we would share Luke's story, we would find others that could relate to his struggles. My mom, sister, brother-in-law, nieces, neph-

> *"Whatever method you choose, find a way to allow your feelings to move from within yourself to outside yourself."*
> *– James Miller*

ews, cousins, and Luke's friends all also experienced great loss in Luke's death. We were all profoundly affected. I have found as I open up and am transparent with others, it allows them to be vulnerable as well, and it brings healing to all of us. James Miller said, "Whatever method you choose, find a way to allow your feelings to move from within yourself to outside yourself."

Long after your friends want to listen, you can journal. My son Jace wrote this on the eleven-month anniversary of Luke going to be with Jesus. It gave me a glimpse into how he has navigated through the loss of his brother. It shows me his beautiful, reflective heart:

"11 months.

How has it been 11 months?

In a sense, it feels like it was only yesterday that he was here; like he could be walking through the door any second with that huge smile.

In another sense, though, it's been a lifetime since he died. I've walked through the deepest valleys, yet at times have felt a more profound joy than I ever had before.

I've been surrounded by the best of friends that care so deeply, and at other times have felt that they've completely forgotten me. Highs are higher, and lows are lower.

Life is more meaningful sometimes, and seems completely pointless at others.

I have a harder time deciding what I want out of life, because it seems to be something that changes every day. One moment I want to be the change that I want to see in this world, while at others I could hardly care less.

Today the rain bears down on me with skies gloomy and darkness looming. Tomorrow the sun shines on me with fresh light and new life blooming.

I used to imagine grief as a linear process:

Unbearable sadness from the start that held an inverse relationship with time. As time passed, sadness would decrease, life would return to normal.

This generally does hold true with grief, with the caveat of having a long enough time horizon.

In the same way, if you were to look at a graph of the stock market for the last 100 years, you would see a very steady upward trend.

Here's the problem with a 100-year graph, though: it doesn't show the day to day struggle. It doesn't show the highs, the lows, the lower lows.

It doesn't show that one week you feel as though you're on top of the world, that the grief has made you stronger, and that you think you're finally ready to move on with your life. It doesn't show the week after that, when you come crashing to your knees yet again, crippled by this loss that you thought had been grieved.

But it's all a part of the twisted, wicked, sacred, beautiful process they call grief.

If it weren't for the rain that came today, there would be nothing to water the grass, the flowers, and the trees. If it weren't for the sunshine that came soon after, there would be no light energy for the plants to photosynthesize.

They're both needed.

Be glad when you have highs; when life starts to make sense again. The sun shines a little brighter, the joy you feel is a little deeper. You're stronger every day.

At the same time, however, endure the lows. Work through them with grace by facing whatever is being thrown at you. Feel; hurt; cry. Talk to someone about them. Write in your journal. Play some guitar. Take a sick day. The lows will pass, and you will see the light brighter than before.

Trust in the process. Trust in the Lord.

This too shall pass."

JACE GOODMAN, AT 20

Jace sat down and wrote that and that same day put it on "reddit. com" a website where people can share thoughts. Someone put it on "best of Reddit," and it went viral—he had over 300,000 hits in 24-hours. That shows me that there are a lot of hurting people out there. We have all known loss in some form or another. It struck a chord in a lot of hearts.

Jace considered taking a finance job in California that an acquaintance offered him as he graduated from ORU—a long way from Oklahoma. In Oklahoma, he had a healthy support system and family and cousins who loved him dearly. He was twenty years old. I remembered my experience after my sister died. I had also just graduated from ORU. I lived in Tulsa and worked in a hospital here after I graduated. I came home from the mission field directly to her hospital bed. As I previously mentioned, I had no support group because I had been gone for five years, and all my high school friends had moved on.

It left me in the most hurting, painful time of my life when my sister died, and I was very vulnerable. I made bad decisions during that time that I would not usually have made. I had to face consequences that lasted decades. I did not want to see Jace have to walk a similar path, getting out to California and knowing no one, having no support group after just having lost his brother. I shared with him my experience but left the decision completely up to him; we would support him in whatever he decided. Thankfully, he chose to stay. He did get an apartment with some buds of his. He had support and love surrounding him that helped him through his early stages of grief.

Later he told me he was so thankful he had decided to stay at that time. Immediately after losing someone you love, it is the time to be gentle with yourself, give yourself lots of grace, and if possible, surround yourself with support. His and Luke's mutual friends had also walked through the loss of Luke. Whether they talked about it or not, they shared that, and that in itself offered strength.

About a year passed, and he and his cousin Daniel, one of his best friends, took a job together doing highway surveillance in California with Pathway. The timing was great. They had each other. They plugged in with some friends they knew in California that had a fantastic sense of community like nothing Jace had even known in Tulsa, and they had the time of their lives out there for a year. When they finished their time with Pathway, Jace decided to stay on for a while in San Diego and moved into a house with six solid guys that loved the Lord. He loved it.

He later decided to move back home for a season. He felt like he really wanted to be there for his younger brothers. It has been an incredible blessing having him home. He and Rob have both set such great examples for their younger brothers to follow, and for that I am grateful. They have been intentional in their friendships and who they have chosen to spend time with. They are growing in their walk with the Lord and in their influence on others. I am so thankful for the place they are at in their lives.

Walking through the grieving process is messy. You never know when a memory will grab you, put you right back in the moment. If you decide to walk through grieving in a raw, real, and vulnerable way, it not only allows you to peel back layers to wholeness, but it will enable others to walk with you. No man is an island; we are so integrally connected with one another. Life is richer, deeper, and more meaningful when we allow others to journey with us, when we allow ourselves to love more deeply, to feel. The pain is also more significant, but, oh, so worth having loved. As they say, "It is better to have loved and lost than never to have loved at all." Give yourself permission to love profoundly and live fully. Permit yourself to feel joy in life.

> *Give yourself permission to love profoundly and live fully.*

Months after losing Luke we had a precious young couple over for dinner. The young man is the son of one of my neighbors, a dear friend. His dream was to compete riding BMX bikes in the Olympics. He was racing from the age of two, traveling nationally to compete. He was a bodybuilder and looked like a Greek god. He was full of life, love, and joy. He had a heart for others, and for the Kingdom. When he grew up, he was accepted through the army to compete and train in the Olympics. Then he was drafted into service in Iraq. The higher-ups found he had been accepted, yet sent. He had to reapply. His acceptance the second time came a week after he was involved in a tragic accident. He was driving a Humvee with a couple of the guys he was in charge of in his unit. One of them was a professing atheist who cussed at him every time he invited his buddy to Bible Study. He kept asking.

They had been awake for two days with no sleep, running back-to-back missions. They were exhausted. He was driving at night and never saw the wire. They hit a roadside bomb and his buddy died. He survived, but with seemingly insurmountable injuries. It was touch-and-go for months whether or not he would survive. He did, but lives with incredible pain every moment of his existence. He has dealt with crushing guilt over why he survived, and his buddy did not. He was ready to meet his Maker, and his friend was not. His friend made his own choices and he was not responsible for his friend's decisions, but he grieved deeply over his loss. His heart ached until he felt it would break.

When they came to dinner, he asked if we dealt with resentment toward the Lord over Luke. Luke made the choice to try the edibles. His choice to overdose led to him pulling the trigger. So many variables could have resulted in a different outcome. Did we feel resentment that the Lord did not step in to help? Protest? The Lord had warned him, and he was disobedient to that. He had stepped out from under his covering.

Years ago, when our family was newly Christian, we went to a Bill Gothard seminar. He talked about a covering of protection that we all have, using the analogy of an umbrella. When kids disobey their parents, they are willfully choosing to step out from under their covering, like stepping out from an umbrella into the elements. That is when we become susceptible to "the darts of the enemy," like pelting rain, as Bill Gothard taught. For a woman, her husband is her covering, and for the man, the Lord is his covering.

Luke's death was the consequence of his sin. The overdose led to paranoia—he was out of his mind. Satan took control of it and Luke succumbed.

I had willfully not gone there in my mind, through all the "if only's" surrounding Luke's tragic death. I had chosen not to dwell there, and I was not struggling with resentment toward anyone else's involvement, let alone the Lord's. This precious young man was struggling with hurt and resentment over the pain he deals with every moment of his life as a result of the accident. He and his beautiful wife have had to walk through the pain and agony together as they journey through PTSD and the overwhelming load of emotions involved with it.

He could have lived his life-long dream. Instead, he deals with excruciating pain that threatens to consume him. I had no answers. Recognizing the Lord's goodness in light of Satan's darkness did not carry any weight. Where was the Lord's goodness? Looking for things to be thankful for seemed inane compared to his journey.

I know we see things differently than our Heavenly Father does. He has an eternal perspective. This young man is carrying intense suffering. He came to complete crisis eight years out and no longer wanted to live. His wife is a gift. His daughter. His baby son. But even his pain—it is a gift. He will be broken to become whole. God is Sovereign. He is at work.

He did nothing wrong. He went to Iraq with a good attitude. He was persecuted for the light he was for the Lord. He loved his guys. He loved Jesus. Oh, the darkness he has had to walk. I found myself feeling like I had no answers and there is no cliché answer. What are the right questions we should be asking?

The Lord allowed it. He is God. He is working in this young man an eternal weight of glory. He needs real answers. How do you trust in a God that is supposed to be good, and yet allowed this to unfold as it did—as it is? Hovering between life and death.

Growing up, when our family was facing some of the most trying times we ever experienced, a friend of my dad said to me, "You need to thank God for the privilege of having to learn to trust in Him." All things work together for good. We have to trust the Lord has a higher plan.

It is in walking through pain and tragedy that we become conformed to the image of Christ. He carried the weight of the world on His shoulders. He became sin for us Who knew no sin. As I previously mentioned, I often listen to Kat Kerr's teaching on YouTube. For the past fourteen years, the Lord has taken her up to Heaven, and she has had countless visitations there. In Heaven, we will know no pain, no suffering. Because this young man has remained faithful to the Lord, I do not doubt that the Lord will use him in mighty ways, both here on Earth as well as in Heaven.

The Lord sees all this differently than how we view it in our limited, carnal minds that live in the here and now. It is on an entirely different scale to the Lord than it is to us. What we value as important, what we think will bring Him glory—riding a BMX bike in the Olympics, how cool is that?! That was not what the Lord had in mind for him. There is something pain and suffering grows in us that nothing else can. In ways, this friend has the wisdom of an old man.

The pain and suffering he and his wife have both walked through at their young ages has given them such a position of power and influence in the Kingdom. The Lord brings the redemption as He works in our lives. Lord, have Your way. I see such beauty in his wife – inward grace she has had to grow in as a result of walking this out with her husband.

In the book *Grace Disguised*, the author, Jerry Sitter, did not do anything wrong, yet in a heartbeat, he lost his wife, his daughter, and his mother when 2,000 pounds of steel wrapped around them. An oncoming vehicle hit them and he lost all of them in an instant. His life was completely, abruptly wrecked, turned inside out and upside down. How does a person recover from that? How in the world did he find the will to live? To go on? Where we turn in our tragedy determines our outcome. We can become bitter, or we can allow the Lord to become our comfort, our strength, our very breath, our all.

> *Where we turn in our tragedy determines our outcome. We can become bitter, or we can allow the Lord to become our comfort, our strength, our very breath, our all.*

In the Song of Solomon in the Bible, towards the end of the love story when the woman has become wise in years, life, and love, she arises, leaning on the arms of her Beloved. Leaning on Jesus. We become whole as we lean deeply into Him, learning deep trust in the Father. Our paths may at times seem impossible, but He promises He never leaves us or forsakes us. He is genuinely concerned with the inward character He is producing in us. Our eternal glory will so far surpass the suffering we have known on Earth.

When we experience hardship and tragedy, we either run from or run to Jesus. When we run to Him, we can lay it all at His feet. He tells us to "Cast all our cares on Him because He cares for us".

(I Peter 5:7) Learn to run to Jesus with everything you face, trust Him with it, and give it to Him.

I choose to trust. I willfully choose not to walk in resentment to the Lord. It is a decision. I want to ask the hard questions. I want all of Him. I want to reflect Him. My friend Becky, who survived a brutal robbery, told her husband, Chris, "I am not the same. I will never be the same." I see His beauty in her. I see His image reflected in those who have learned and chosen to embrace the pain and yet walk with Jesus.

The young man, Jerry Sitter, Becky—they did not do anything wrong to bring on the random tragedy they all experienced. But their lives are forever changed. The Lord is at work in their souls. They have to learn to lean into the Father. Leaning on the arms of their Beloved.

Leaning, in spite of not understanding how the Father, who they loved and trusted, could allow the tragedy. Leaning on and trusting Him when it is beyond their understanding. Our ways are not His ways. His thoughts are higher than our thoughts.

The Lord has great Kingdom responsibility for every one of

us that have suffered loss and still chosen to trust him. Thank Him for the privilege of having to learn to trust in Him. It is not in vain.

We were at the wedding of one of Rob's friend's a couple of months after Luke died. They played one of the songs we used at Luke's memorial service. Greg, Jace, Rob, and I locked arms, stood there, and sobbed—at a wedding!

So many people ask us how we are doing. We are walking through it. The pain is incredible, but we don't dwell in it. We walk through it to peace and even joy the Father brings. We are not going this alone. We are surrounded by Him, our love for one another, family, and amazing friends that carry us and are there for us. If you do not have the support group you need, ask the Father to bring others to you. Ask Him to give you divine contacts. Often others that have known loss can relate immediately to your pain. These are the people that have ministered to me the most. I am drawn to them like a magnet. There seems to be an immediate bond when someone has gone through a tragedy similar to yours.

I am so incredibly grateful for friends that have been willing to be there for me. I couldn't have made it without them. They give life meaning. The greatest gift you can give another person in their time of loss is a listening ear. I have watched others in their time of grieving that are unable to deal with anything other than the immensity of their loss. I realized that was how I was when I lost my son. It took everything in me to cope in a healthy way, so I had nothing left to offer anyone else for a season. The woman just diagnosed with breast cancer, the man who lost his job two years before retirement, the young girl who witnessed her young sister be run over by a car, the friend and single mom who lost her only son—all have known pain that is all consuming, pain that requires everything in us to simply cope. It is in this time that others become the hands and feet of Jesus. They are an absolute lifeline breathing hope and love into us.

As we allow ourselves to ride the waves of the highest highs and the lowest lows, we find we eventually emerge, feeling like we can once again come up for air. After my son died, I found that I needed to find meaning in every interaction. We have "family night" on Sunday evenings. We have dinner, talk, laugh, play some music or some games, and maybe watch a movie together. Family night is one of the highlights of the week for all of us. Our sons that have left home and gone off to college appreciate it more and more. After Luke died, I found I needed meaning in the time we spent together. It was no longer enough just to be together and enjoy the richness of our time with one another. I wanted and needed to know where everyone's hearts were, how their hearts were, what their highs were, as well as their lows. We needed one another more than we ever had before. It was so satisfying to have conversation open up and have one of us verbalize the angst and acknowledge out loud the myriad of feelings that we were all experiencing. The more real we were in sharing our hearts, the more we all benefitted. We need one another.

Each morning in my devotions, after I write in my thankful

journal, read my Bible, and pray, I pull, from various sources, rich writings that fill my soul. My dad passed away 20 years ago. One of my greatest treasures is his well-worn Dake's Bible. One of his dreams was to publish a book one day of all these great one-liners. He would mostly gather them from sermons over the years, and he always wrote them in the blank pages in the back of his Bible. They do not always flow together, but they all have richness to them. A month after Luke died, I wrote in my journal these thoughts from Daddy's Dake's:

"Where you turn in your time of weakness will determine your failure or success."

"Always give Me credit for everything. I will lead you into the places you would never think to go. I will give you the strength to do it."

"Joy is the surest sign of the presence of God."

"He gave us two eyes to see, two ears to hear and one mouth to speak. Oh, that we would have eyes to see your goodness. You love us through our eyes as we hunt for Your goodness. We should be listening—to You and others twice as much as we are speaking."

"You give us Peace like manna. We need it every single day. Every minute of every day. We receive it when we come to You with prayer, petition, worship, and thanksgiving."

"Don't pray for the Lord to use you, pray that He makes you usable."

And then on that same day, I copied this down from Ann Voskamp's *One Thousand Gifts*:

"Who am I to see glory with unveiled face? Is that what the child seeks? And me, slowing for the hunt, sanctuaries in moments, seeking the fullest life that births out of the darkest emptiness all the miracle of eucharisteo (thankfulness)."

"Who can gather the manna but once, hoarding and storing away substance in the mind for all of the living?"

Like my dad and Ann, I have found I have to get my manna from the Lord every single day. He brings me great joy as I read from great minds and grab hold of pearls of wisdom.

The next day in my journal was one month from the day Luke died. It was overcast and rainy, which matched how I felt that day: somewhat despondent. I had friends calling, reaching out to me, and loving me from across the miles. My former college roommate, Chrissy, sent me a plaque with Luke's picture on it, saying at the bottom, "Born April 16, 1992." Below that, it read, "Lives forever with our King and Savior, Lord Jesus." My friend Susan sent me a scrapbook she had made with all our kids together since birth. She called and reminded me of a funny story. She was babysitting Luke, who was two at the time. Her two-year-old daughter Shannon was pulling animal crackers out of the kitchen cupboard. Susan looked at her and told her no. No response. The look from Mom. "Shannon . . ." Luke looked at Shannon and said, "First time (obedience) Shannon, FIRST TIME." Susan cracked up laughing.

My friend Carrie Kittinger came over on that same day and loved me by being there for me. We walked three or four miles and had such a meaningful conversation. She gave me a wall hanging that said, "It is well with my soul." My neighbor Kristi brought us two loaves of zucchini bread and left them in my mailbox. I thought of the saying, "Friends remind us of our heart's song when we forget how to sing it." Oh, I am so thankful for friends. They are like the hands and feet of Jesus to me.

4/23/15:

Psalms 141:8 But my eyes are toward You, O God the Lord; in You do I trust and take refuge; pour not out my life nor leave it destitute and bare.

Psalms 16:11 You will show me the path of life; in Your presence is fullness of joy, at Your right hand there are pleasures forevermore.

Psalms 18:6, 2 In my distress I called upon the Lord, and cried to my God; He heard my voice out of His temple, and my cry came before Him, to His ears. The Lord is my Rock, my Fortress, and my Deliverer, my God, my keen and firm strength; in Whom will I trust and take refuge, my Shield, and the Horn of my salvation, my High Tower.

Hebrews 2:13 And again He says, My trust and assured reliance and confident hope shall be fixed in Him, and yet again, Here I am, I and the children God has given me.

Isaiah 8:18 Behold, I and the children whom the Lord has given me (even Luke) are for signs and for wonders that are to take place in Israel (I have heard it said America is the new Israel) from the Lord of Hosts Who dwells in Mount Zion.

4/24/15:

My heart was ripping out and broken last night seeing Jace trying to take senior pictures for his ORU graduation and the sadness/despair in his eyes that was not there before. His soul is in pain. It broke my heart.

I called him after and we sobbed together on the phone. This morning we both feel fragile, vulnerable. Father, cover him with Your love, Your grace, Yourself. Help him know Your arms. Bring peace to his soul. Father God, I trust You with my life. I trust You to get me through grieving Luke.

Luke won't be here for Jace's graduation, which would also have been his own. He won't be able to be the best man in Jace's wedding. To be a groomsman in Rob's.

I won't see him marry, have children. I won't see him fulfill his purpose, his calling, his destiny for You. His life is snuffed out.

He is with You. Lives forever with our God, our King, our Savior.

Be still and know that I am God.

4/28/15:

Lamentations 3:22–26 It is of the Lord's mercies and lov-ing-kindness that we are not consumed, because His (tender) compassions fail not.

They are new every morning, great and abundant is Your sta-bility and faithfulness.

The Lord is my portion or share says my living being;

therefore, will I hope in Him and expectantly wait for Him.

The Lord is good to those who hopefully and expectantly wait for Him, to those who seek Him (inquire of and for Him and require Him by right of necessity and on the authority of God's word).

It is good that one should hope and wait quietly for the salvation (the safety and ease of the Lord).

Psalms 34:8 Oh taste and see that the Lord (our God) is good! Blessed (happy; fortunate, to be envied) is the man who trusts and takes refuge in Him.

Numbers 11:1 And the people grumbled and deplored their hardships which was evil in the ears of the Lord.

Father God, help me not grumble and complain. Help me trust in you in this temporary loss of Luke, until we are with him again in glory. Help me see with Your eyes. Speak to me. Sustain me. Guide me. You are my hope. You are my refuge. You are my strong tower. In You I trust. I will not be overwhelmed, crushed, consumed by grief.

You are my rock, Oh God. May the God of hope fill you with joy and peace as you trust in Him that you may overflow with hope through the power of the Holy Spirit. Romans 15:13

Psalms 62:8b Pour out your hearts to Him, for God is our refuge.

May 4, 2015:

Ephesians 3:16 May He grant you out of the rich treasury of His glory to be strengthened and reinforced with mighty power in the inner man by the (Holy) Spirit (Himself indwelling your innermost being and personality).

Ravi Zacharias was the graduation speaker at Luke, Jace, and Daniel's graduation yesterday. He said in his speech, "We are not a body with a soul. We are a soul with a body."

The only way I will make it through this whole is to cling to You, Father. The lower I bow to You, the more intimacy I have with You.

I journal separately from my thankful journal. These are some of the entries in my thankful journal which overlap with the above dates:

526 I am thankful that Greg and I are learning to parent from the heart and not behavior.

527 Morning sun on snow-capped mountain peaks

528 Vail vacation with Greg, Luke, Chad, Seth, and Joy

529 I am thankful Jace has a job he loves

530 Rob's missions trip to Peru this week

531 I am thankful that the hearts of my children love You!

532 I am thankful for Your goodness even in Luke's death (this was my first thankfulness journal entry after Luke graduated to Heaven)

533 that the body of Christ has overwhelmed us with their love in so many tangible ways

534 for getting to be with Luke at his bedside in CO until they took him to be an organ donor

535 I am so thankful that I got to kiss and kiss him, and lay my head on his chest for hours and listen to his heartbeat

537 for Your comfort

538 that Rob made it home from Peru for us to tell him before anyone could randomly let him know, or he could hear of it on social media that his brother shot himself

Rob was arriving home at 5:30 pm from his missions' trip, ready to change the world, on the day we found out at 2:20 in the morning about Luke's death. We could tell no one all day, lest word get out before we let him know. Can you imagine him finding out on social media? Whew!

539 I am thankful for Vicki — working, planting, giving of herself and her talents planting flowers in the flower pots all over my back deck

540 Alisa picking up Luke posters for the funeral service

541 Jake running Greg's errands so that he doesn't have to

542 I am thankful for all the women in Mom's Bible study — cooking food for an army, and for their prayers for us.

543 Kim Winn's church — brisket, love, and massive amounts of food

544 Alisa and Marley, Kelsey and Alli and their friends cleaning my house

545 You, Father, anticipating every need!

546 Paul and Kathy bringing fruit, Dean and Carolyn bringing dinner

547 Bobbi shopping for dresses for me for the funeral service and bringing me five to pick one from!

548 Love, Love, love! Thank-you Jesus! I feel your love!

549 My devotion this morning from Jesus Calling on Trusting You that You are taking care of me. That You have given me Your peace that You want me to walk in.

550 Shared tears mingling with Greg's over Luke

*551 I am so thankful for messages from friends that are holding us
up in prayer – they are our Aaron and Hur*

In the Bible, they held up Moses arms when he could no
longer hold them up. As long as his arms were up, the Israelites
were winning the battle.

552 for the tenderness of my children

*553 Jesus, I thank you that this massive blown up poster board of
Luke that we did for the Memorial service is ministering comfort and strength to me. I look into Luke's eyes of love, and I
see You. His smile is completely captivating, and it warms my
soul. It captured his dimple that I have kissed a thousand times.*

555 I am thankful for the love of my husband!

*556 I am so grateful for love-making and the joy, intimacy, love,
and laughter that goes with it.*

557 the good night sleep that almost always follows it.

> *Making Love*
> *A holy*
> *Act*
> *Of worship*
> *The union*
> *Of two souls*
> *In vulnerable*
> *Intimacy*
> *Beautiful pleasure*

Sometimes the very act of making love, the intimacy of it,
brings tears to my eyes for the beautiful gift that it is. If you have

lost your spouse, then you will well remember the beauty of that gift. There are many couples that have lost a child that lose interest in making love with their spouse, when this is one of the greatest ways of bringing healing to your soul. If that is the case, examine what is behind that. Are you blaming your spouse? Do you harbor unforgiveness toward them related to the death of your child? The enemy would love to divide you and destroy your family. Jesus tells us to forgive.

558 for the love of friends

559 the hundreds of friends that have reached out to us since Luke's death

560 (Easter) I am so thankful for Your resurrection after conquering death, hell, and the grave!

561 You are risen!

562 I am so thankful for Your overwhelming love!

563 I am so thankful for Your attention to the minutest details of our lives. You provided even the food we needed for Austin— when we are going to see Greg's parents, Natalie and Bob. I haven't been to Walmart in a month, nor am I up to going yet, but I have had every single food item for this trip – to cookies for Greg, snacks, and meals that I usually always prepare. You overwhelm me.

564 for seas of Texas bluebonnets, wildflowers waving in the grasses

In the middle of my thankful journal, sometime quite before Luke died, at this place, I had skipped ahead and written this:

What pain and suffering have you had to endure in your life that brought you to the place where you are today?

566 *I am thankful that You love me, you are for me. That song continually has run in my brain since You gave it to us 3–4 times in the car on the way home from Colorado the morning we left Luke.*

574 *I am thankful that Luke spent his final days, weeks, months enjoying life and living it to the fullest.*

575 *that You use us to give in our most profound pain if we allow You to*

576 *that giving brings healing*

577 *that we didn't have to see years of dark drug abuse with Luke*

578 *Thank You for healing hugs.*

584 *Hundreds' of exquisite iris's lining the driveway that I transplanted over eight moves from our Kansas home; in Heaven, we won't have the weeds also*

586 *I am thankful that Luke died knowing that he was fully loved.*

589 *that I never had any premonition of losing Luke*

599 *leaves clapping in the wind on trees*

600 *eyes to see Your goodness*

601 *the continual gift of Your peace*

602 *boys and girl humming hymns*

603 *laughter*

604 *gorgeous smiles*

606 *tears*

607 *memories*

608 *my family*

609 *Your presence and Your realness in our lives*

610 *emotions*

611 dimples

612 Greg throwing my towel over the top of the shower for me, so I don't have to open the door and get cold grabbing it.

613 that even in the ache of missing Luke I sense his warmth, his love enveloping me—or is that You? He was like You in love

615 for perceptive friends

616 for Carrie Kittinger and our wonderful soul refreshing walk/ talk today

617 Kristi Rhodes giving me two loaves zucchini bread today—on Luke's one month since he relocated to Heaven day

618 grey skies to match my sad heart today

621 one hour talk with Jenny

622 My friends are gifts. They lift me up.

625 I am thankful for this year of firsts ahead, missing Luke at every turn.

626 Joy stopping school and plopping in my lap when it is time for hugs and kisses.

628 Our hot tub—the greatest place to solve all the problems of the world.

631 Seth laying his head on my shoulder

632 Vicki giving me a massive Kimberly Queen fern yesterday

633 that we are finally having John and Charica Daugherty and family over for dinner tonight

635 juicy ripe mangoes!

636 sharing them with Chad, Seth and Joy

637 Yvonne giving me a complimentary massage

638 I am thankful that when I am overwhelmed, I can run to You!

639 the brilliant red feathers on a cardinal

643 Jace walking into our church this morning and surprising us! His big, beautiful grin and hug.

644 Jace giving us his day—church, lunch, dinner

645 Family time

647 competitive ping-pong

648 pond time with the family

651 guitar time. Rob teaching Jace, Greg joining in

652 (like my daddy used to say) "Here we are, taking up ALL this space! – in Rob's room – on the floor, bed, chair, closet, lounging, hanging, connecting, cherishing the moments together. Refilling our cups. Our hearts. Our souls.

653 that Your mercies are new every morning

654 Jaime Boefferding saying last night that Luke always made her feel like a million bucks

This thankful journal has enabled me to navigate through the seasons of grief with a grateful heart. Our Lord knew the difference it would make in our hearts and lives to give thanks in all things. It enlarges our heart and our soul. He commanded us to do that for us, for how it would impact us. It helps us keep our focus on Him, the Giver of all good things. Waking up each morning and thinking of all the things I am thankful for in the day before has helped me not miss the gifts. So many would slip by unnoticed if they were not named. This has been my greatest secret on navigating through grief.

GRACE IN GRIEF

"The trials and the suffering are working toward
a consuming glory."

Come Away My Beloved

T he apostle Paul wrote almost half the books in the New Testament. Paul suffered many hardships, trials, and afflictions. He knew much of God's grace. He begins and ends many of his letters, now books of the New Testament, with, "Grace be with you, be with your spirit…" (Philemon 3). The Amplified Bible translates grace as "God's favor and spiritual blessing." 2 Thessalonians 1:2 reads, "Grace (unmerited favor) be to you and heart peace from God the Father and the Lord Jesus Christ, the Messiah, the anointed one." Grace is unmerited favor—like my favorite worship song, "Reckless Love" says, "Oh the overwhelming, all consuming, reckless love of God—we didn't earn it, we don't deserve it; still, He gives Himself away." His love is reckless because He took a chance, with great risk, on loving us.

149

It is in suffering and pain we learn to give ourselves and others grace, as we experience and know the grace of our Heavenly Father. Colossians 1:2 states, "Grace and heart peace from God our Father." Father sounds like such a protective, comforting word. If you did not know that from your earthly father, it is hard to understand and see how that translates in how you view your Heavenly Father. Webster's defines "father" as, "protector, provider, creator, founder or author of; to originate, to assume as one's own." We are His. He takes us as His own. We came from Him. Grace and heart peace—these two go together in this verse. Heart peace comes when we walk in His grace. Our Heavenly Father is crazy about us. He delights in us. My lifetime verse

> *It is in suffering and pain we learn to give ourselves and others grace, as we experience and know the grace of our Heavenly Father.*

is, "He will keep in perfect peace whose mind is stayed on Thee, whose heart trusts in Thee." (Isaiah 26:3). I say that over and over, meditating on it. To have heart peace or perfect peace, we have to train ourselves to keep our mind and our thoughts focused on Jesus. And then we relinquish ourselves to Him. Abandon ourselves, if you will, to Him. No matter what comes, we know we can and will trust in Him.

I need to digress here to make a point. My dad passed away when I was 34. He had some unresolved anger toward his own dad, who he mistakenly believed all his life had abandoned him as a child. My dad was a passionate, wonderful, loving man, but his unresolved anger led to rage in his own life. I remember as a teenager reading about the Lord being gracious, compassionate, and slow to anger. What?! Slow to anger? That did not compute in my mind because my dad was quick to anger. I could not grasp the concept that my Heavenly Father was slow to anger because my earthly father was not. We tend to view our Heavenly Father in light of our earthly father. Our earthly fathers, unlike our Heavenly Father, are far from perfect. He wants us to know, deep, deep within ourselves of His amazing grace and love for us. He wants to fill and heal the void left in our hearts and lives from the father that raised us. We base our image of ourselves on our earthly father, but our true identity comes from our Heavenly Father. We are His sons and daughters.

In her book, *One Thousand Gifts*, Ann Voskamp wrestles with suffering and God's grace. She says, "It is suffering that has the realest possibility to bear down and deliver grace." She continues, "Grief transfigures into grace, empty transfigures into full. God wastes nothing—makes everything work out according to His plan." He truly wastes nothing. He uses this suffering and pain to produce His grace in us. We can allow the Lord to produce growth in our character through our loss. Through it, He molds us to become more like Him. We become agents of His grace as we empty ourselves to become full of Him. I have found that I can extend so much grace to others because of the deep pain and loss I have known.

She goes on to explain the meaning of "eucharisteo." When Jesus fed the disciples the last supper, he blessed the bread and gave thanks, which translates to eucharisteo. She breaks down the word so we can see—charis=grace; eucharisteo=thanksgiving; chara=joy. We begin to transform our thinking by thanking Him in the hard things, for the hard things. She says, "Eucharisteo always precedes the miracle." We give thanks. We name the gifts He has given us. Our Father then removes the layers off the eyes of our heart to see and know His grace, and we find joy. Thanksgiving leads to our heart peace, so it is well within us. Giving thanks comes before we know joy. The miracle, for us, after knowing deep pain, is deep joy. Heart peace with deep joy. This . . . is grace in grief.

Since journaling was so instrumental for me in grieving with grace, I want to share with you more of my journey. As I look back, I see His grace covering me in this season:

8/17/15 from *Come Away My Beloved*—I will prepare within you a different attitude of mind. Thoughts that have been in confusion, I will reorganize. I will not bring to bear upon you pressures that will cause you to be weak. I will be to you the strength you need. I will be to you the inner fortification which will bear you up even in the time of strain and crisis.

Saturate your soul in the oil of the Holy Spirit, and keep your channel of communication ever open to your Heavenly Father. His desire is toward you, and He will be your strong habitation.

8/19/15 Psalms 131:2 Surely, I have calmed and quieted my soul like a weaned child with his mother; like a weaned child is my soul within me (ceased from fretting).

Psalms 37:7 Be still and rest in the Lord; wait for Him and patiently stay yourself upon Him.

8/23/15 Five months ago today Luke died. We have all cried today. Sometimes I just hug – like Seth today. There are no words. No words of comfort. It just hurts. I hurt in the center of my soul. My chest aches for Luke.

Seth was so sober over lunch. No words, just one tear.

My thoughts of Luke warm me. His smile melts me still in my mind. His warmth. His embrace. His smell. His essence.

Jace walked in church this am and I was exhilarated. I was so thrilled to have him. The next verse we sang was, "You give and take away. You give and take away. My heart will choose to say blessed be Your name."

In fractions of a second, I went from joyful over Jace to tears of Luke.

8/24/15 Thank you, Father, that You are my peace. In Your presence is fullness of joy.

8/25/15 Father God, help me to view every day as the gift from You that it is. As I name gifts from You, awaken me to the fullness of Your love for me. You are the giver of all good gifts, the lover of my soul. Awaken me to Your glory. Give me eyes to see, ears to hear. Hold me close today, Father.

8/26/15 You brought Chris (Luke's best friend) home for a reason. Father God, I love to see how You provide.

You are my peace. In the world, you will have tribulation. You are our strength. To the cross I cling. Now is the time to rise up in You. To walk in Your peace. To be unshaken by the events going on around us. "Great peace have they that love the law of the Lord and nothing shall offend them." Psalms 119:165, KJV

8/27/15 Psalms 63:7,8 For You have been my help, and in the shadow of Your wings will I rejoice. My whole being follows hard after You; Your right hand upholds me.

8/28/15 From Ann Voskamp: The humble live surprised. The humble live by joy.

"Is it only when our lives are emptied that we are surprised by how truly full our lives were?"

I came home from Colorado trip with Luke thanking God for His goodness in our lives — so thankful for our family and where we were as a family. Help me to see it now, Father. In the day to day living, to revel in the fullness of the life You have given us.

Ann Voskamp, like me, also has six children, similar in age to mine. She has homeschooled her children as we have.

Ann – "The world I live in is loud and blurring and toilets plug and I get speeding tickets and the dog gets sick all over the back step and I forget everything and these six kids lean hard into me all day to teach and raise and lead and I fail hard and there are real souls that are at stake and how long do I really have to figure out how to live full of grace, full of joy – before these six beautiful children fly the coop and my mothering days fold up quiet?

How do you open the eyes to see how to take the daily, domestic, workday vortex and invert it into the dome of an everyday cathedral?"

I am just bawling reading that.

9/22/15 We are healed of a suffering only by experiencing it in full. Marcel Proust

And then from Kenneth Haugk in *Experiencing Grief*: You can't think your way through grief, you have to feel your way. You can only heal what you feel.

> *"Don't depend on others to permit you to grieve – give that permission to yourself." – Kenneth Haugk, Experiencing Grief*

He goes on to say, "Don't fight the horse or try to control him. Simply move along with him and let him take you wherever he wants to go." It is the same with grief. Experience the feelings stirred up by your loss. Share the painful memories, and talk about the issues that surface.

"Don't depend on others to permit you to grieve – give that permission to yourself."

"Perhaps the most important truth I have learned is that healing in grief is heart-based, not head-based." Alan Wolfelt, *Understanding Your Grief.*

2292 I am thankful for spectacular sunrises

2294 I am thankful Luke went on to be with the Lord instead of being in a vegetative state for the rest of his life.

2295 I am thankful not to be responsible for $250 K in medical bills that would have caused us to acquire.

2296 I am thankful Luke would always tell Joy, "Love you long-time!" He still loves her from Heaven.

2305 *That you bring me joy in You and in knowing a glimpse of what Luke is experiencing in Heaven, where there is no sorrow. There is no pain.*

2306 *Greg playing pickleball with me. The fun of exercising together.*

2307 *That You have become my High Tower and Defense, and my God, the Rock of my refuge. Ps. 94:22*

2313 *Toni's warm, welcoming love and acceptance*

2314 *Shelley's precious heart, love, and understanding. You wrap me in Your love through friends like Shelley and Toni.*

2315 *Peace in the storm*

2316 *Sally just texted me, "I am filled with gratitude for our friendship... I am thinking of you today. Wow! What a plan God has for you.*

2317 *For the letter we got from Cheryl, Luke's pancreas recipient. If it is the only letter we receive, it is enough. It was everything I would want in a recipient letter.*

2324 *That there is beauty in loss*

2325 *I am thankful that even in the darkness of loss, we find others with whom we can share life together.*

2341 *Thank You that I can come to You and fill my cup every morning. Thank you that Your mercies are new every morning. I find it hilarious, Your sense of humor, that most mornings You woo me out of bed with a hot flash. I throw off the covers, and then I look at the clock, time to get up to be with You, and so I decide to go ahead and get up to have my devotion.*

2344 Breathtaking sunset at ORU last night for the 50th reunion. It revealed the GLORY of God! You showing Your blessing over ORU.

2345 Serenity; the power of the full moon through the trees last night as I was coming through the gate. I had to stop and take a picture.

2346 I am thankful for my delightful Turkey Mountain hike and visit with Melissa, what a jewel she is!

2347 That we get to go to their son's soccer game with them tonight at ORU

2348 That Melissa and Chuck were in the stands and Chuck was filming when Davis got his first collegiate goal! They were in from Oregon to see him. He was put in the game and scored within a minute and a half! That is so like You, Father! What a gift! Thank You, Jesus! Thank You for caring about the intimate details of our lives.

2358 Charla praying with Giovanna for our family and praying for laughter and joy bubbling up – specifically for Jace. We both experienced exactly that, him yesterday me this past week! Thank You for the absolute deep knowing of Your incredible love for us. They prayed it for us. We both experienced it!

2359 Overwhelmed by Your love

2367 Delicious family time – being together! The kids all loving on one another. Building one another up. Jace and Rob encouraging Chad about his debate in class today.

2368 Jace and Rob caring enough about Chad to come to watch Chad do his debate today.

2369 *Rob buying Chad 'gin-gins' (ginger candy he loves) and ginger beer after his debate today and telling him he NAILED IT!*

2370 *Your sense of humor. You used a harlot to keep the two Israelite spies' safe that were sent in to survey the land in the Bible. You preserved her and all of her household, family, extended family. Everyone matters to You.*

2371 *That Jace landed safely from skydiving*

2376 *Greg buying me Poison (perfume) today. No occasion! Just because.*

2380 *I am so thankful that I can turn to You every minute of every day.*

2385 *That You carry me when I am overwhelmed*

2386 *I am thankful that you give us natural remedies to healing sickness in our bodies – herbs, essential oils, foods with healing properties, pressure points*

2388 *For the thousand endless jobs that give me the opportunity to be the blessing, to become the gift*

2389 *For friends that understand and give me grace*

2390 *For Donnie and Shawna bringing their entire relation to you. To NewSpring (church) yesterday.*

2391 *For the light in Shawna's eyes yesterday*

2392 *For beautiful, rich sermons*

2395 *I am so thankful for our relationship with Jace (21) that has so blossomed since Luke died. He confides in Greg and me both. He asks for counsel. He uses such wisdom in looking to You for answers. I am so incredibly grateful.*

2396 Joy's butterfly the other day. It walked to her and climbed on her foot, letting her hold it for 45 minutes! Then it fluttered to my chest and rested there. It deeply moved her.
2407 For two date nights with Greg this week

It seems as I look back at my journal during this time, I see what I imagine many experience after losing a loved one. I go from walking in peace and joy, to at times feeling so sad I feel I could hardly move. Our family lives a crazy, busy life with our Kettle Corn business, especially during our most demanding months in the spring and fall. After experiencing tragedy or loss, it is not the time to add on a momentous change in your life. That first fall after losing Luke, we added a food truck to our already crazy season. I was working our second largest event of the year in another city with several of our children while coordinating a thousand details related to equipping a new food truck: the menu, supplies, and the 24 workers needed for the weekend.

I realize now, looking back, those times of pure exhaustion were when I cratered the most deeply. When I was physically and mentally exhausted, it was so much more difficult to cope with our loss. I became sick with the flu and run down, yet had to keep going and keep performing. The more you can build in downtime during these seasons, the more it will help you cope with the loss.

I have come to realize how important it is not to compare ourselves in this season with others and their productivity. They are most likely in a completely different season of their lives, and sometimes the most spiritual thing we can do is allow ourselves time to rest. This is where grace comes in. Give yourself and those around you grace to grieve.

∽

Around the six-month mark after Luke's relocation to Heaven, I wrote a note to him:

9/28/15 Luke, I feel this overwhelming sadness I don't know how to shake. I look at the poster headshot of you we had made for your service and there is such a consuming beautiful love you reach me with.

I am not motivated to do all I need to do for four kettle corn events this week. I don't care about any of it. Your daddy doesn't seem to like me too much these days. Less sexual interest than ever. He went to Austin to see Baboo and Grand on the 22nd, and for the first time, it was a relief to have him gone.

I don't know where my joy has gone. I need, more than ever, to cultivate my thankful heart. I have struggled as much through this six-month mark as I have since you died.

I have this deep-seated sadness in my soul. Nothing touches the waters of it. I miss your fun bantering with your brothers. I still occasionally imagine you coming into the kitchen. Sauntering in. "Hi Mama."

Jace sent me a text tonight asking a question. When I didn't respond, he said, "Mom – quick!" And then, "Mahm!"

Cracked me up. Reminded me of you.

I can't but smile when I look at your beautiful smile and dimple. I love you, Luke. I am thankful I so often told you that. You knew you were deeply loved.

You are deeply missed. Our lives are off kilter, and we don't know how to "aright" them.

And then, some days later:

9/30/15 Jesus, You are my lifeline. I only live in peace and fullness when I am resting in You. Give me eyes to see.

Don't just take the blessing, be the blessing.

Jesus, use me to bring Your light and Your life. Keep my focus on You alone. You are my rock, my strength, my fortress, my God in Whom will I trust.

10/1/15 "We shall steer safely through every storm, so long as our heart is right, our intention fervent, our courage steadfast, and our trust fixed on God." St. Francis de Sales

10/6/15 Light is sown for the righteous and strewn along their pathway. And for the upright in heart, the irrepressible joy which comes from consciousness of His favor and protection. Ps. 97:11

"Every person who truly, deeply shares your pain with you is doing God's work." *A Time to Grieve,* Kenneth Hauck

"Stand still, and whisper God's name, and listen. He is closer than you think." Max Lucado

In the next journal entry I made, I find it interesting looking back and seeing where I was in the grief process. I think the thoughts I experienced are common to many in the grieving process.

10/11 Last night was Swan and Jackie's wedding. Luke would have been a groomsman. I did not struggle as badly about Luke not being there as I had anticipated. I saw him in my mind as a groomsman.

I feel so disjointed in life. I have a hard time engaging—even when, like last night, everyone is there that I love. Help me to fully, fully love. Help me, Jesus, to be all there, all present—with Greg, with my children. I drove to and fro with Greg to the wedding without connecting with him last night. Help me engage with who I am with in each moment. Help me value others.

I struggle with people never mentioning Luke. Never bringing up his name. Last night at the wedding someone walked up to me and said, "I just saw Luke in the parking lot!" Then his eyes widened, and he quickly corrected himself, "I meant Jace!" I think he was mortified. I wasn't. I know others are thinking of him, they just never tell me. I feel like everyone has gone on and forgotten him as though he never existed. I need his friends to talk about him.

I know what Rob meant when he said he was afraid to do life without him. I am afraid to let go of his memory, as though I am not honoring him, or doing him justice to do life without him.

He is gone. I do want to be whole again. I still feel like part of me is not there wherever I am.

Jesus, Oh, how I miss him. How's he doing in Heaven there with You? He knows what he has left behind, yet he is there with You. It is infinitely so much better being with You. He doesn't experience sorrow or tears, yet he has an awareness of the ache we feel in missing him.

At something like the wedding last night, I feel guilty if I leave Luke out of it, if I enjoy it and have fun without giving him a place, Father. Yet it was good to be able to do that. Father, I let go of that. I see it – the guilt, and I let it go.

Embrace the living. Say or do the things with our other five children that I would pour into Luke.

Letting go of guilt is a key to your healing. It is okay to go on, Kim. It is okay to keep living, loving, pouring into others. Yes, it is all different. It is like I have an amputated limb. But people learn to live, to choose life, choose joy, and be overcomers even with amputated limbs. Some days I am ready for that. Most days I am not.

Father, though I know Luke isn't there, his ashes are all that is left of him physically. Sometimes it is comforting just to hold them. When it is no longer comforting, I will be ready to spread them.

10/13/15 Cheryl (the woman who is the recipient of Luke's pancreas) put a hummingbird on Luke's letter she sent and inside it said, "Hummingbirds (which I love!) float free of time carrying our hopes for love, joy, and celebration. The hummingbird's delicate grace reminds us that life is rich, beauty is everywhere, every personal connection has meaning, and that laughter is life's sweetest creation."

That so resonates with how I believe! Your beauty is everywhere! Thank you, my Jesus!

Jerry Sitter—*A Grace Disguised* – soulful people love. If people want their souls to grow through loss, they must eventually decide to love even more deeply than they did before.

Jesus, help me not become emotionally distant from my children or husband. Help me embrace them, love them more deeply.

Jerry Sitter tells the story of a woman who lost her mom when she was ten went to counseling when she was twenty for the loss of her dad, who was still alive. Because of his loss, he became so emotionally distant. Help me be all here. All present.

Ann Voskamp: Spend the whole of your one wild and beautiful life investing in many lives, and God simply will not be outdone.

10/14/15 Jesus Calling: Joy emerges from the ashes of adversity through your trust and thankfulness.

10/15/15 Luke's Instagram: Follower of Christ. ORU graduate. Boarder of everything. Thrower of Frisbees. Seeker of life.

10/22/15 Today Alli (my sister) would be 50! How different life would have been had she lived. She was such a giver. Father God, help me embrace life, choose love this day. Help me wear love. I praise You this day. I choose to praise You.

Today was the day seven months ago we found out that Luke shot himself.

Thank You for Alli and Luke in my life. Thank you for their short lives and the impact upon my soul and others they made. I choose to walk in Your joy despite the pain. Heal the physical pain that this is. Today is seven months since the son—the boy grown man, the baby who opened my womb went to be with You, Father God.

He was standing on the brink of manhood.

Grief is crushing today.

10/25 Give us this day our daily bread. Not just the physical – it is the manna you give me every day I live, to thrive. My sustenance. You are my sustenance.

10/28/15 My depths are held by peace. The surface may be disturbed; it's the depths that count. Stanley Jones

10/30/15 A gentle tongue (with its healing power) is a tree of life, but willful contrariness in it breaks down the spirit. Proverbs 15:4

A man has joy in making an apt answer, and a word spoken at the right moment, how good it is! Proverbs 15:23

Father, help my words bring life and edify others. Help me use them to build others up, encourage and strengthen. Help me be a wise woman who builds her house.

The tongue of the wise brings healing. Proverbs 12:18b

A good man shall eat good from the fruit of his mouth. He who guards his mouth keeps his life. Proverbs 13:2, 3a

2418 that You are with us this Thanksgiving when Luke cannot be.

On Thanksgiving Day, I wrote: Just got out the china to set the table for the Thanksgiving meal. I took out eight place settings. Realizing what I had done, I just set them down and retreated to my room and bawled. Jesus, I miss Luke so badly!!! It just doesn't want to convert in my brain that there are seven of us now.

I need meaning out of today. So far, a parade and the kids are all playing Mario Kart video games all morning.

I don't know if anyone is aware Luke is not with us! Greg just came in to love on me and hug on me.

I am so grateful to have our beautiful family at the breakfast table today. Lively. Full of life and love and laughter. Yet I am so missing my Luke!

It is raining. It is good to have rain today on this first Thanksgiving with no Luke. Rain is all of Heaven crying with me.

2419 *Claudia, Shelley, Janet and Jill all reaching out to me yesterday – it's been 8 months since Luke was relocated to Heaven.*

2420 *Thank you, my Father God for laying us on the hearts and minds of others to pray for us, and for them letting us know it. I really needed that yesterday. I am so grateful to You.*

2421 *Claudia telling me that she has prayed for Luke every day since the day she met him years ago. Wow. That is mind-blowing. Thank You Jesus.*

2423 *That our relationships have become more meaningful with one another since Luke died.*

2424 *That every single one of us gets to be together today on Thanksgiving Day—all of the Fowler's, Goodman's, and Mom (all 25 of us, Caren and other close friends). We had sweet family time with our own family on our first Thanksgiving without Luke before going to the Fowler's.*

2427 *Your goodness in the land of the living.*

2428 *My bedroom view.*

2429 *Vibrant color of fall – exquisite trees.*

2430 *Our cozy bed.*

2431 *My husband that loves me and I adore and respect.*

2432 *Waking up slowly.*

2433 *The flavor of Earl Gray tea with Sucanat and cream.*

2435 *The recipient's that are alive today because of Luke's organs.*

2436 *All the other recipient's that have benefitted from his skin, his tendons, ligaments, eyes, bone.*

2442 *Trudy saying to me yesterday, "You might as well know how fond I am of you… I feel like I've been to Bible Study when I'm around you. You are an angel."*

From *Come Away My Beloved*, His joy springs forth most abundantly in souls that have been soaked in tears.

2468 *Delicious, homey evening with family, fire in the fireplace, Christmas movie.*

2469 *Greg and Joy's sweet cuddling in the green chair eating fruit snacks and precious conversation.*

2470 *The Christmas season, Your season, to slow down and honor and give thanks to You for the Christ child.*

2471 *The most glorious sunrise this morning. For 15 minutes the color was exquisite!*

2472 *That I got to have a dream about Luke last night!*

2477 *Jace saying last night as we put together the Christmas card for 2015—cruise in January with Luke, and then Easter picture three weeks after Luke's death, "Mom, let's not use that picture, let's use a more recent one. For about four months after*

Luke's death, I forgot how to smile...But that is not where we are anymore."

2487 The universe. We are studying Your vast and awesome universe in science. Mind-blowing!

2497 Daniel's Christmas post about deeply trusting You — You are our oxygen, loving others. Love is the only thing with eternal value—how we love others.

2516 Geese flying over and honking

2539 That though this was the hardest year of my life, it was beautiful, full of life, meaning, growth, and You.

From July 2017: One day I was thinking of what Luke would say to me if we had a conversation now.

Luke: Mom, I love you, but there is no way I could have come back. I can't wait for you to be here with me. Mom, Jesus loves you so much. It is amazing being in His presence. There is no way to describe the overwhelming peace, the joy I now know. I never know angst, only pure joy and the love of the Father. He is using me in Heaven. I am completely fulfilled. Completely whole. Live out your earthly life Kingdom focused. You have an eternal reward waiting for you.

When we get to the throne room to worship Abba, our hearts are full to overflowing. I am busy in Heaven doing His work, but never, never rushed. I minister in peace. I have even been taking voice lessons! Can you believe it? I play Heavenly instruments and am training to be leading worship. I am about my Father's business.

168

Jesus is my best friend. He shows up and is beside me when I am thinking of Him all the time. I have had the most phenomenal times with Him. Mom, when I was on earth, I smoked pot to try to experience Him on this deep level. I was wrong to do that. My spirit and soul craved Him. Now He meets me constantly. Now even when He is not there, I am always aware of His presence with me.

You always said our purpose was to know Jesus and to make Him known. I know Him, Mom. Be still in His presence. He wants intimacy with you now. Don't crowd Him out. He is the most important thing.

I am fulfilled. I am whole. Long before you see me, He will be using me on missions to those still on earth. It is an incredible honor to be used that way. Granddad is often used that way. You know. You were with him in dreams before I left you.

2/16/18 I had been experiencing tightness in my chest that at times escalated to feeling like I was having a heart attack. Last night Greg prayed with passion for me. "Father, help Kim! Help her return to normal!"

Simple. Two lines. Prayed with passion. With those simple two lines, You answered. Pain and tightness that I had been having in my chest for a week that was increasing ceased immediately.

It is gone today. Even that vulnerable feeling of weakness like I had just had an 'episode' is gone today. Praying is an art today.

People get together for hours of intercessory prayer. Jesus said, "When you pray, don't pray as the Pharisees with long-winded prayer. Two simple sentences and You answered. Thank You, Father!

With passion pray.

With passion, live.

With passion work.

With passion make love.

I am finding You answer our prayers when we pray for others. It seems not so much when we pray for ourselves. Prayer connects us to You and others. You use the passion and prayers of others to be an extension of You to us.

3/17/18 Jesus Calling: Rejoice in the One who understands you completely and loves You perfectly.

I am now in the 5,000's.

5170 Being on a cruise with Bob at 96 years of age. Greg making it happen.

5171 Last night at dinner I asked Bob (my father-in-law) what he felt contributed to 65 years of a great marriage with Natalie. The main thing he shared was that he chose to listen to Natalie, her input, to not always have to be boss. He loved and respected her. Thank you for the example they have been.

5172 Later he turned to me and said, "Y'all have a great marriage. (28 years) To what would you attribute a great marriage?" Wow! What an honor he said that to me.

Jesus as the center.

Choosing where to park our thoughts. Choosing to have a grateful spirit, not to hold grudges, to allow the other to be human and love them as they are.

Our heart and soul connect times and getting on the same page – hot tub times, the greatest way to solve all the problems in the world.

Regular date times to enjoy, delight in one another, and not talk about the kids.

Frequent lovemaking.

5278 *I am thankful Rob did not become paralyzed in Belize as I later learned he dove from five feet off the water into 2 ½ feet of murky water after his GoPro he had accidentally flung out into the water. Thank you! Thank you, Father! Thank you for Your guardian angels You post around us!*

5338 *I am thankful for my cousin Caren moving here from Virginia and becoming an integral part of our lives.*

5339 *Toni and David celebrating 33 years of marriage together for their anniversary. They have a marriage that will impact the world. She sent out a post saying that everything they are is because of the Cross. How incredibly poignant that their 33rd anniversary fell on Good Friday – the same age Jesus was when He went to the Cross.*

5340 *How these seeming numerical coincidences are no coincidence to You. Numbers are so significant to You. You laid out the Universe numerically. You hold our earth in orbit at a precise quadrillionth fraction of a distance from the sun.*

5341 *That Toni and David have ten kids, seven sons, three daughters, just like Job in the Bible had before he lost his family, and in the one You gave him after his trials. Wow. They have gone through fire and trials, different than his, but like him.*

5342 *I am so thankful to be able to do life with my sister Toni. I feel this holy reverence reading her book as I am beginning to understand, maybe more so than her right now, how her book is going to rock the world. It is Your message to Christians around the world to help them overcome and truly learn how to Thrive as You want us to do.*

5343 *I am thankful that thousands of people are seeing Victory Church Easter production this weekend. It is anointed, and You are using it for Your glory.*

5344 *I am thankful for the anointing that is on John Daugherty to write these plays for Easter and Christmas to help Christian's break out of their narrow religious paradigms—such a beautiful way to see those walls beginning to crumble. I am so thankful Rob got to play the role of Peter with John playing the role of Jesus. It was incredible. John later told me this had been a dream of his for years!*

5345 *Seeing You at work using the body of Christ to get Your message out, to help us think as You think, live as You want us to live*

5346 *Mom reminding me of a dream last night that Toni had after Alli died. In it, Alli said to her, "I can't wait for you to meet my Jesus! He is so much fun!!" This is the Jesus that John por-*

trayed in the Easter production last night. Jesus that, unlike so many other times he is portrayed, is charismatic, fun loving, a people magnet that everyone clamored to be around. He was full of life and love and color—the Jesus we all want to follow.
5442 *Thank you, Father, for the majesty of the storm*

>*The power of the wind*
>*The Heavenlies reverberating with rolling thunder*
>*The sound of birds awakening the morning*
>*The soft rain pattering gently*
>*After its fierce pelting in the night*
>*The comfort of the sound*
>*The Holy hushed Reverence surrounding me*

⤜⤛

I have shared with you my day to day so that you can see what this journey looks like. There are times when it is just messy when walking out grief. Sometimes we take it from minute to minute or second to second; we are holding on and walking this out, our humanness covered with His grace. In the journey, I have found that when we are brave enough to face the pain of our loss head-on, to embrace the emotions, the hurt, and the grief, it loses its power over us.

Because we all grieve differently, there is no magic formula, certain time period, or right or wrong concerning grieving. The important thing is that you give yourself and others grace to grieve for as long as it takes. And then, when you think you are all finished grieving, something may hit you and you need to do more grieving. Such is grace.

RELEASING YOUR LOVED ONE

At the one year day from Luke's death, we faced the decision whether we as a family would return to our newly acquired timeshare in Vail to again spend a week with the family where we spent our last with Luke the previous year. I was not sure I would be able to handle it emotionally. I couldn't even imagine walking into the condo where we spent Luke's final day with him. I knew if we did, it would be an emotionally loaded week, and I was not sure I was ready for it. We attempted to sell the week. We put it before the Lord and told Him that we would trust His will and if it did not sell, we would know that He would bring new layers of healing to our hearts. Jace had never even been to the condo. He had been working the previous year as a new college graduate and had been unable to make the trip.

As it would turn out, we all went as a family and had a phenomenal week together. We made new memories and enjoyed

175

having a blast together. Even in the fun, there was a poignant awareness of our loss.

Throughout the entire year since Luke's loss, I would often share thoughts with the family. Like I said, I read every book on dealing with grief and walking through loss that I could get my hands on. I learned so much, and I was intentional about sharing these nuggets with my family to help all of us process our loss. Unless we are intentional in facing our grief and embracing the pain of our loss, we cannot become whole. I would often share from a book I was reading with my family and then it would open up rich discussions that we all needed to experience and share with one another.

I previously mentioned that when my younger sister Alli died, I had no one to help walk me through my grief. I had no idea how to do that. Because of my experience, I wanted all of us to be able to talk about our feelings and share our hearts with one another. I did not want to see my children go through what I did so I became intentional in sharing to open our hearts and allow us to verbalize the emotions and feelings we were all carrying within us. It drew us closer as a family.

The grief counselor at our church told me that even Jace and Rob at their ages when Luke died, 20 and 18, would have tools in their emotional arsenal to deal with losing Luke that their younger siblings Chad (13), Seth (12), and Joy (7) would not have, simply because they were too young. I found that I had to verbalize thoughts and feelings for Chad, Seth, and Joy because they were not able to. I would put words to the overwhelming emotions they wrestled with, and cause them to think through, work through and even sort through their thoughts.

In the car on this trip to Vail, I had just read something, and I said to the family, "Can I share something with y'all?" Jace piped up from the back seat and said, "No, Mom. I just need to let Luke go." He needed a break from processing through emotion. This was the trip where one year previously we had spent our final week here on earth with Luke. Everything inside of me was screaming that I needed to be able to shoulder that with our family, yet that was not at all where Jace was. We all process through grief differently and that has to be ok with us to allow our loved ones to do that in their way. I had to give Jace the grace he needed. Needless to say, that shut me down. That was Saturday.

Over the next few days, we made new memories together. We played together, laughed together, snow skied, and snowboarded together. We did not mention Luke's name. I had thoughts and memories to think through, as we all did. Wednesday night at dinner, I again asked if I could share a few thoughts. By then we were relaxed and wanting to talk. After I read from my journal, Jace was the one that took the lead, opened the discussion up wide, and began sharing his heart.

We had Luke cremated. I grew up thinking that Christians did not do that because we believe that when Jesus returns, Christian's will rise from their graves to meet the Lord in the air, and how could they do that if their bodies were ashes? I have read the Bible through from cover to cover over twenty times in my walk with the Lord. I have never found anything that supports that. I came to understand that our Creator God is certainly not limited as our finite minds imagine. It is not our mortal bodies that meet Him, but our immortal bodies, which are already in Heaven with Him anyway!! Our physical bodies are only a shell of our spirit man that goes to be with the Lord immediately when we depart this earth.

We had decided we were going to spread Luke's ashes in three places doing things he loved most—on the ski slopes, out at the lake where we spent countless hours out in the boat in the summers as a family, and off the back of a cruise ship that we will one day take together again as a family. Luke was an entity in the front of the boat. He always worked out his schedule to join us as a family when we went out on the boat. I could only remember one time when we were ever out in it that he was not able to join us.

On Wednesday night in Vail, we all decided we were ready to spread Luke's ashes on Thursday. I said, "So, do we want to ski into the woods and find a quiet place together so we can have a ceremony for Luke?" Rob said, "No way, Mom! Top of the mountain for Luke!!" I laughed and said, "Of course! That would be so fitting!".

The next morning, we all took the lift to the highest point on the mountain. Even our little Joy, who was seven, ascended to the top. Of course, she skies down faster than I do! We got off the lift and skied straight across, staying high up on the mountain. I shared first what a friend of mine had texted me for us that morning – she prayed for us that when we speak to others, we focus on living the fullest life for You, wrapped up in the greatest joy and adventure of serving You. Satan always has a counterfeit of deepest joy in walking out this incredible journey with the Lord.

I also shared from Isaiah 61. The Spirit of the Sovereign Lord is on me because me because the Lord has anointed me to preach good news to the poor. He has sent me to bind up the broken-hearted, to proclaim freedom from the captives and release from darkness for the prisoners (Satan has such a dark grip on people's minds, edibles – lead people into terrible darkness), to proclaim the year of the Lord's favor (we had certainly known that this past year) and the day of vengeance of our God (He will avenge the enemy – vengeance will come as we fight back – as He fights the battle with/for us), to comfort all who mourn (because we have known deep grief this past year, and great mourning – yet He will take us and use us to walk others through their pain – even in ours. He will use us to comfort others. Pain is every-where – but where there is pain, there is grace), and to provide for those who grieve in Zion. To bestow on them a crown of beauty instead of ashes, (wow, we were literally spreading his ashes) the oil of gladness instead of mourning, and a garment of praise instead of a spirit of despair.

I said that I want to remember God's goodness to us this past year, and how He so carried us and loved us through His body. Now, He sends us to bind up the brokenhearted, to proclaim freedom for the captives, and release from darkness for the prisoners. And, we pray that He redeem Luke's death in the way we all live out our lives.

I shared how the Lord had done all that for us throughout this previous year and commissioned us to allow Him to work healing in the lives of others who had known loss because of what He had done in our lives. Jace spoke up and said, "That is not what I need from this Mom. I need this to be a time of release. I need to be able to release Luke." We all also agreed that we needed that from this time as well.

I handed Luke's ashes to Greg to spread. They were in a small cylinder canister. Instead of spreading them out before us as I would have expected, Greg spread them up into the air above us, and they rained down on us through our tears. It was so perfect. His ashes were skin colored, not gray as I would have thought. I looked down at Seth's boarding boots, and they were covered in Luke's ashes. Then we locked arms in a tight circle, hugged one another, and then prayed—a raw, from the heart, beautiful prayer together. We acknowledged that Luke was among us and that Heaven was touching earth that day as we prayed. It was all perfect. It was exactly what we needed.

Typically, when we are skiing down from the top of a long run on a Colorado mountain, we ski down a couple hills, stop and catch our breath, look down at the next hill or two, plot our course in our mind, ski down that, wait for one another to catch up, and then continue down the mountain. Ok, so usually they are all waiting on me... Luke was an absolute daredevil on his board. As I mentioned previously, he literally would be boarding ahead of me as he turned circles going down the mountain while carrying on a conversation. He would find every jump and bold move and take it.

After we prayed and cried together at the top, Greg said, "Let's ski this one down for Luke!" Every one of us took off and skied the entire way to the bottom of the mountain full speed ahead, never pausing once until we hit the ski lift at the very bottom. It was the most exhilarating, freeing, fastest run I have ever done. I don't think I would do it again. We were going crazy fast. It became symbolically and literally such a time of release for each of us. Something happened within each of us that day. We all experienced the release Jace talked about at the top of the mountain.

In the Bible when Abraham died, his family grieved him for a full year. In our culture, I believe people don't allow themselves to grieve, and they have to be able to do that to become whole again. Because we allowed ourselves to embrace our loss and then allowed ourselves to release Luke, we have been able to know joy and peace within our hearts. The Lord is restoring a radiant heart within us. That is something only the Father can work in us. We give Him our brokenness, our hurt, our sorrow, and our pain, and in exchange He heals us, restores us, comforts us, and delivers us.

> *We give Him our brokenness, our hurt, our sorrow, and our pain, and in exchange He heals us, restores us, comforts us, and delivers us.*

There was something so powerful for each of us in our immediate family in being able to "release" Luke. During the first year after he died, he was always on my mind. Throughout my days it was as though I experienced life through this "Luke" lens. It was all I could think about. Each month anniversary that first year was so difficult and so all-consuming for me. We all needed to be able to let him go. Many that have walked this journey of losing a loved one feel they are not true to their loved one if they release them or let them go. Many feel guilty about moving on with their lives and feel they are almost betraying their loved one to do so. It was the most freeing thing in the world to release Luke.

In the second year, the dates of the 21st–23rd that I so struggled with in the first year would go by, and I wouldn't always even realize it. Your loved one by no means wants you to stay in bondage to his or her memory. If your loved one truly loved you, and if you truly loved them, the healthiest thing you can do is to let go of them. Look around you at the friends, family, and loved ones you have in your life now. They need you to move on; they need you to deal with the pain of your loss so you can live again. Your loved one would want you to be free to live, to love, to joy in life and in others. I give you permission to let them go. Give yourself permission.

That time of release may look different for everyone. I couldn't even take Luke off my lock screen on my phone for over a year and a half. I chose not to do that until I was ready. We will never fully get over losing Luke. He is an integral part of the tapestry of our life. He will always be a part of us, as will your loved one. Letting go comes in stages. The important thing is to allow yourself to do that—to let go. We found that release on the ski slope. Ask the Lord to show you what that key is for you. To show you what will unlock that release for you or your family. I have heard of people writing a letter of release to their loved one and sending it up in a hot air balloon. One friend, whose son had committed suicide, had a party on her son's birthday and invited his friends to all do a balloon release together for him. This was cathartic not only for her, but for all of his friends as well. Whatever that release looks like for you, whether it is literally or figuratively, whether in a ceremony, or a place you loved and shared together, it is an essential piece of this puzzle involved in the healing process.

Recently our family was at the lake celebrating Jace's 24th birthday with friends of his. One of his friend's, Lauren, was telling me that she has known several families that have lost a child. She shared with me, "Your family is the only family I know that have lost a child that doesn't wear their grief—where you look in their eyes and see they have known sorrow." She said, "I know you will always carry the loss of him, but you don't wear it." Because we were able to release him, we are free to move on to celebrate the joys that are before us.

I have seen people that have lost a child cry to talk about their loss over thirty years later. It is all okay. At that point, grief is not all-consuming, but the mention of their child can tug at their hearts and bring fresh tears. Know that this is okay. Early on, it is a day by day process. Releasing someone you have held so dear does not always happen all at once. But I know for us, it was a huge part of our healing. When the time is right for you, it is absolutely freeing to give yourself permission and to give yourself the grace, to release them.

COMMEMORATING YOUR LOVED ONE

"Prayers for my Fowler/Goodman brothers and their families, please. It amazes me the amount of evil in the world that everyone seems to overlook. Luke was one of the best guys I had the privilege of hanging around, and I am so thankful for that. He was always quick-witted and sharp and could make you look stupid reeeal quick if you weren't on your game. He was always fun to be around. I honestly never saw him upset, unless I beat him in poker! This group of men, brothers, and cousins, are people I have always admired. I've looked at their family bond and wished I was a part of it. To be honest, I think the devil really messed up on this one. This band of brothers is not someone I would want to mess with. To you, men, may you be strengthened in this time and take back what the enemy stole from you. I pray you have strength that surpasses understanding. And that the bond between your two families would only grow deeper. I pray your spirit be enraged, like mine, against the enemy and you go hard against him. I love you all, my second family."

Daniel Carney

On the one year anniversary of Luke's homecoming with Jesus, we decided to have a service in our home to commemorate him. This again, was a huge part of our healing process. We had our family, both Jace and Rob's girlfriends, my mother, all of my sister's family, and Luke's lifetime best friend Chris join us.

We had just returned from our ski trip to Vail. I was talking with Greg and asking him what he would like for the service. We thought we would open in prayer, and then have everyone share memories of Luke that they would like to share. Finally, we would close with showing the slideshow that we had put together for Luke's memorial service, since none of us, including myself, had gotten to see it because we were in the back room together beforehand when it was showing. We had it showing for the first thirty minutes as people came in.

My nephew, Caleb had called as we returned from the trip and asked if he could have a time with all Luke's closest friends on the 21st, which was the day Luke shot himself. We decided to have our time at our home on the 23rd, as that was the date on his death certificate. I would love to have been a fly on the wall at Caleb's service. I knew that was not my time to share, but I would love to have heard the memories shared. Jace said it was an incredibly emotional time.

Our service in our home did not necessarily go as planned but thank the Lord, that is how He works. He had different plans for it. Greg opened with the most powerful, poignant, raw prayer I have ever heard him pray. It showed so much growth in him that he experienced in our past year. The evening became a time rather than sharing memories of Luke, of what the Lord had done in each of us since his passing. We all shared our journey and the ways we had been impacted and the process that the Lord had brought us through. It was a sacred evening. We closed by showing the slideshow as we cried and laughed together. Even though it was different than we had planned, it was everything we needed it to be.

After we returned from our trip to Vail, Jace shared with his cousin Daniel (who was one of Luke's closest cousins and his same age, 22) about our time of releasing Luke on the mountain. That inspired Daniel to write the following and experience his own meaningful time of releasing Luke. It is long, but it shows how he has journeyed losing his lifetime friend and one of his closest cousins. It shows how he commemorated Luke.

Losing Luke

BY DANIEL MICHAEL FOWLER

One year ago today, my cousin, Luke Goodman, took his life after consuming a form of edible marijuana that was legally sold in the state of Colorado at a dispensary. He took much more than the suggested dose because he didn't feel the effects until he had taken too much. In a moment of mental torment, he made a rash decision which would forever impact his family and hundreds of friends.

I've not spent time writing of him much apart from my journal. This is not meant to be an inspirational piece, nor is it my way of memorializing him as I did at his funeral shortly after his death. These are my thoughts, my questions, my feelings, and my lessons after his death.

Losing Luke was probably the hardest thing I've ever gone through. I was very close to him and grew up with him. I have countless memories of him and seem to recall him multiple times a day, from one thing or another. I often hush the memory for another time, but sometimes when I am feeling extra vulnerable, I open up my mind and my heart to all of the feelings and memories of Luke. I was discussing with Jace (Luke's younger brother) today of how deep I would have to dig just to open myself up to this letter.

I've realized I had three favorite things about Luke, outside of what most people remember.

1. He was never on his phone when he was around people.
2. He was always a yes man, ready to do anything.
3. He left his legacy in the people who knew him. Don't let his legacy die in you.

In the last year, I have questioned things I never thought I might question. I have allowed myself to re-examine the grit: Why am I here? What is worth my time? What am I supposed to do? Where am I supposed to live? Who do I want to be? Who is God? To what extent does He love? What role do I play in His story?

I've watched how this has broken and remolded my entire family (Fowler's and Goodman's) together and individually. How do you walk on when you carry the life of another on your shoulders? My motivation has always been something I've prided myself in; I used to be the hardest worker in the room. I worked my tail off through ORU, pouring myself fully into my studies, graduating with a 3.94 in Finance. I vested into the RA program and went on to become a head RA. I poured myself into missions and led a team of 10 to Chili for a month in 2013. I worked five of my eight college weekends as a student there. I took on more than almost any student I knew. And in one crashing instant, all accomplishments seemed to fall away as nothing, meaningless. There are different levels of value, and I had made the mistake of putting all of my efforts into a value lower than that of the highest level. Since Luke died, I seem to have no motivation to do anything. I have jumped from one thing that I am doing to the next, finishing nothing along the way, always having my "reasoning" for jumping to the next thing. The truth of it all is that there is a question coming from within, 'what if I succeed in something, I finish, and find that it provides me with no answers, it offers me no future hope for satisfaction or fulfillment, it gives me no feeling of contentment or purpose with which to jump to the next thing?' What if the platform I jump to sinks, and I vested enough into it that I sink with it? For if I finish, I have no more excuses as to why my purpose remains empty. I have no reason that my cup shouldn't be full and overflowing. Therefore, I inhibit myself along the way subconsciously. I maybe allow or even cause myself to fail, holding on to a parachute, never allowing myself to jump into freedom.

Ravi Zacharias was the keynote speaker at my graduation ceremony from ORU. I have since listened to his podcasts often. In a podcast of his, he refers to the story of Eric Liddell and of his rival Harold Abrahams. Near the beginning of the movie when Harold Abrahams is asked by a fellow competitor, "How does it feel to lose?" he responds with pride in his voice, "I wouldn't know, I've never lost." After Liddell decides to not compete in his main event in the Olympic games (100-meter dash) because it falls on the Sabbath, Abrahams is asked by the same fellow as before a different question, "Do you fear losing Harold?" to which Harold responds in a most peculiar way. He says, "Aubrey, I've known the fear of losing but now I am almost too frightened to win. I will raise my eyes and look down that corridor; 4 feet wide, with ten lonely seconds to justify my whole existence. But will it?" It is not the fear of failure that is most paralyzing, but rather the fear of succeeding and finding out that everything you have worked for did not fill the void in your soul, nor did it succeed in offering satisfaction for all of your toil.

See, I realize what Solomon meant when he said, "Everything is meaningless." Why do we toil under the sun for everything which falls away? I've found that grief sets in as a weight upon my shoulders, something I cannot shake off, for I have chosen to walk with it. Seneca, in his 22nd letter to Lucilius says, "Search the minds of those who cry down what they have desired, who talk about escaping from things which they are unable to do without; you will comprehend that they are lingering of their own free will in a situation which they declare they find it hard and wretched to endure. It is so, my dear Lucilius; there are a few men whom slavery holds fast, but there are many more who hold fast to slavery."

I've discovered that I am holding the very straps to the burden that I call grief. For I fear that upon letting go, I lose my last part of Luke, something I've not the stomach, nor the heart to lose.

So, the question with which I now grapple flips itself on me. Do I have the courage to abandon my ropes, lose my burden and walk in the freedom which He died for? For isn't that why He died? To give us an identity not dependent on how we succeed, what we do, how righteous we live, who we know, how much money we make, where all we go, how much we know or how close we are to perfection. Upon sifting through my questions, I realized that that is even more of the victory which Christ died for upon the cross. He bears the burden; He literally holds onto Luke for me. I can rest in the fact that Luke is not released, never to be seen again, torn away from me and the rest of his family. But instead, he is held in the mighty hands of the Father, he rests in Him, he will never depart from Him again. Losing Luke has made me reexamine the redemption I have received in Christ. It has made me ask "What then is this love? What does this freedom free me from? Who am I in this identity which He offers?

I was not liberated to be bound by something, I, therefore, have come to recognize that I am not bound by grief because He offers the solution. Not only is He forever holding Luke in His hands, but we will see him again, which means He is good, for only He who is good can make such things as death good. Only He who is Lord of the universe sees our last breath before we take it, only He who created the universe can change the very laws of nature, only He who provided Moses his law, can then fulfill and abolish that law with his own: Grace. Do you know what this means for you and me? It means that as He makes all things good, that as death loses its power, as the law is abolished and sin no longer can keep us from Him, as His very own son provided our redemption without any bit of our say in the matter, that as His love literally burst through the laws of the universe to capture my heart and pull me into His arms, this means that the eternal life that He comes to offer me is neither limited to everlasting (outside of time), nor is it limited to heaven (outside of space) but is actually eternal in that He wants every bit of me (and you) in every second of our existence, before we were born and after we fall away from this earth. For what is eternal life but this, to know the Father and the Son?

The grief which I hold, the straps to my burden, my need for success, motivation and achievement, I cannot hold onto one without holding onto all. For upon the full realization of the Grace and Redemption of the cross, all of them fall away, for they are one and the same. As truth reveals himself to the seeker, it is not an answer to a question which he reveals, but instead, it is the embrace of one lover to another. As truth has offered me this freedom, I am once again pulled on by this lover, the romantic of my heart who guides me to see that the only thing binding me, in this life and beyond, is my own fear of freedom in its fullness. So, to anyone reading this I ask of you, 'what ropes are you holding onto? What noose are you making for yourself? Ask yourself if you fear the very gift He gives you due to the unlimited possibility to which you might rise or from which you might fall. The life he offers is not the one of perfection which we imagine, nor is it of being ultimately good. No, it is of life...taking place in the Kingdom of Life, outside and separate from the kingdom of the knowledge of good and evil, or of judgment, or of the law.

Thank you Lord for making all things good, for using death to bring life, it can only be done by you. Therefore, to conclude this letter, to you my dear Luke, beloved of God, confidant, brother, friend, Son and healer...I release you.

⌘

Finding a way to commemorate your loved is a very significant step in your healing process. You may not write a masterpiece (like my nephew) of his thoughts on what his journey has looked like in wrestling and grappling with the big questions of life as a result of losing his cousin, and one of his best friends. But he had the courage to compile his thoughts in an incredible, real, raw way, and confront them head-on as he so beautifully expressed.

Commemorating your loved one is often prompted by a special occasion, such as a one year anniversary, their birthday, or another important date you shared. Find a way to commemorate them with those they loved, and that loved them. It may be a service, or it may be as simple as setting a place at the table and sharing memories at a special meal or lighting a candle in honor of them on a special occasion. You may use recipes of a grandmother that has passed away to make Christmas dinner for the family so everyone can enjoy Grandma's pecan pie and her marshmallow sweet potatoes. You may want to write a letter honoring what they meant to you, how they impacted your life and others. If you have a service for them with other family members or friends, you may want to have everyone come prepared to share something meaningful about them, or what they loved about them.

We have sayings we love to use around our home that were things Granddad used to say. He would say, "Here we are taking up ALL this space" when we were huddled together in a stairway talking, or, "I love you this much", showing no room between two fingers like he used to tease his oldest grandson. We often start a sentence, "Like Granddad used to say…" and that from the granddaughter that never knew Granddad. It is a fun way to keep his memory alive.

My younger sister Alli that died when she was twenty-one loved making crafts. She made me Christmas ornaments by hand that take a special place on my tree each year. She even painted "Joy" on one of them, thirty-three years before we had a daughter named Joy. Once when Joy was a toddler, I was telling her about her Aunt Alli that she never knew. She looked me in the eyes and said, "I know Alli." Hmmm. Selah.

In our journey, we found it so healing to share with others that had been deeply impacted by Luke's life and death. Our pain had been so great that it was difficult to understand how deeply others could be hurting over his loss. We are not alone in our pain, and it brings healing to others and ourselves to be able to share that with one another.

I find comfort in wearing one of Luke's shirts. I particularly like to wear them when we work a Kettle Corn event because that is a time that he would have been with us. I often see him in the mannerisms or expressions of his brothers. Both Chad and Seth learned to solve the Rubik's cube on the day of Luke's memorial service, inspired by him. Chad has gone on to solve a five by five Rubik's cube instead of three by three. It makes me think of him as I watch them solve it.

My dear friend, Sally recently shared with me her family's tradition of commemorating or remembering her dad. The entire family relation goes to his graveside on Memorial Day each year to remember his legacy. They bring a picnic lunch to the graveside. They laugh and cry as they tell stories of her dad, lessons they learned from him, how he impacted each of their lives. It is an incredibly special day for all of them. It is a tradition that is very healing for them. It is a way her mom, family, siblings, and children have found to honor her dad. It is comforting to all of them.

I have talked with and known many people that are afraid to let go of their loved one because in so doing they feel they are not faithful to their loved one. As Daniel wrote, 'what ropes are you holding onto?' Our loved one is now with the Father, walking in complete freedom and joy, and wants us to be free to experience the same. Commemorating them is a time to honor them, to remember them, to share with others that also knew and loved them. It frees us to let go. We are still here. We still have life to live, others to touch, love, and influence, wonders to see and experience. Commemorating your loved one can allow you to do just that—to release them, to let them go. No guilt, but truly letting go.

The timing of this differs for everyone. For us, this was at one year. It may look different for you, but I encourage you to find a way, your way, that this works for you. It may be on the date of a special occasion or holiday. It may be one year after their death, every year, ten years later, or any number of ways. For our family, we found it an important stepping stone for us in our journey back to wholeness.

A dear friend of mine, who is a single mom, lost her 24-year old son to suicide several months ago. I did not know her before that. We have become close as a result of what we have both walked through. She has decided each month, on the anniversary of his death in this first year, to do something to commemorate him, something also to get her out of her comfort zone and show her son she is willing to get beyond her fears. I admire her greatly. Last month, she got a group together and fed the homeless. This month she is taking a group of twelve friends to do indoor skydiving. Wow! I love how she has chosen to commemorate him. It inspires her, gives her something to think about that is positive and is stretching who she is as an individual. Great idea! It is helping her to go on living when the one she loved so deeply, her only son, is gone.

My friend that lost her 17-year old son found a way in every family Christmas card their family sent out for years to include some remembrance of her son Caleb. One time, she included his basketball shoes. Other times she and the family insert something else that speaks "Caleb" to all of them. It was one of their unique ways they chose to commemorate their son.

At the three-year mark of Luke's home-going with the Lord, we were wanting to share time as a family commemorating him. Rob, our third son, was again on a mission trip for spring break and this time to Guatemala. We decided to wait until his return, take an evening to hear all about his week, and then have an evening honoring Luke. He returned to a very hectic week filled with play practice each night until midnight and after, and it wasn't until after the Easter production play a week later that he had time to catch his breath and even unpack from his trip.

I have learned to walk in peace and trust the Lord's timing. It was good he did not have to walk in the door from the mission field and commemorate Luke since he heard on his previous mission trip about his brother's death right as he walked in the door. It was a good thing not to again make that association with a mission trip, and the Lord knew that. As a family, we decided to wait until Luke's birthday three weeks later and have the special time together then as a family.

As I write, he would be 26 today. So, last night, for family night, we shared a time to remember Luke. I cooked his favorite meal he would have requested for his birthday meal, which included shrimp with cocktail sauce. We laughed together remembering a trip we took when he was five years old. We stayed on the Disney property. They had an "all you can eat" buffet. Luke filled his plate to overflowing 4 -5 inches high with shrimp. It looked bigger than he was. He returned to the buffet not once, but twice, and did the same thing and proceeded to eat every bit of it.

When he went to be with the Lord, I had put away, rather than giving away, to special friends, cousins, and brothers, like I did with many of his things, clothing and other articles that were "SO Luke" for all our family. I pulled these things out for the first time last night. I watched his brothers do what I had done, sniff his clothing to see if it still smelled like Luke. It did not. It was a such a walk down memory lane for all of us because we could all picture him in his well-loved clothing. Among these items included shorts he had confiscated from his best friend Chris, a jacket that he kept that was another friend's – Christian, which was way too small even at the time of the funeral to return, and much-beloved sweatpants that he acquired from another friend, Kyle, despite Kyle's protests and telling him he wanted his $90 sweatpants back! Luke wore them until they were worn out.

We had a special evening of sharing. As I have mentioned, I am usually upbeat. Last night, however, I wanted to encourage everyone to share from their heart about where they are in their journey in losing Luke and what they think about now, three years later. I intentionally started the conversation with a story sharing with the family an area I had struggled in about Luke. It was good because it set the tone and allowed everyone to follow suit. After we had all shared, I then asked if they had a memory of him they wanted to share. I started with a funny memory. We laughed and we cried together over the next hour or so sharing memories.

Joy wanted to watch a family video together and she picked one where Luke was nine years old. We watched him and Jace recite a long poem they had memorized in homeschool. We watched them play the piano. Jace read the music as he played, and we realized Luke was not able to as he played. We marveled at his love for K'nex and his brilliance at putting together his 10,000 pieces, "Power Tower Crane" complete with motors, that he had gotten for Christmas that year. He was giving me a tour on video of that and the many other K'nex creations he put together all by himself. It was a great evening. It was meaningful and what we all needed.

I shared in detail in hopes that it brings ideas to mind for your times commemorating your loved one. Each time for us will be completely different. We may choose different occasions, or even different locations, to remember him. One year we may have some of his close friends over and let others share stories.

I encourage you to find a way or ways to commemorate your loved one. It is a way to honor their memory. If you do not have an immediate family you could share this time with; you can reach out to someone that is close to you and take the time to share with them your heart and your thoughts on your loved one. You may want to reach out to someone who may also be grieving the loss of your loved one. We had some friends that gifted us a tree to plant in Luke's honor. I chose and planted my favorite – a crabapple tree. He died on the first day of spring, which has always been my favorite time of year for all the life and color it brings. The crabapple tree blooms beautifully in the spring. It is an exceptional way for me to remember him. It was an incredibly thoughtful gift that keeps on giving. You may want to write a letter or a poem to your loved one. On your loved one's birthday, you may want to bake his/her favorite cake, cook his/her favorite foods, and talk and laugh and sometimes cry as you remember him/her. Find a way to remind yourself and your loved ones that he/she will always be a part of who you are as a family and that your loved one will forever be in your hearts.

BEING INTENTIONAL IN YOUR THOUGHT LIFE

"Many of you have heard of the loss of the precious young man Luke Goodman. It is impossible for most of us to wrap our hearts and heads around what our dear friends are walking through today. Luke Goodman was an incredible young man who inspired so many. Though we don't understand, we can be motivated to dream about Heaven, challenged to mark with purpose this temporary time we have on earth and deeply driven to love as Jesus loves. Please join me in prayer for the incredible families of the Goodman's and the Fowler's. There are not many who are around these families who have not been changed through their intentional friendships and their heart to love deeply those God places in their path. Their faith in God is strong. They are hopeful that Luke's life will be an inspiration to his generation. But even for the strongest in faith, their arms need to be held and each word, prayer, and memory will add strength to theirs. Though we see through a glass dimly, one day we will see clearly. I do believe with all of my heart, that Luke's life will be a seed for his generation. A seed to live with clarity of purpose. A seed for a burning zeal to know Christ. And a seed to abandon all to love all that He loves."

Kim Ford

I touched on this concept in the chapter on choosing thankfulness, but I want to expound on it. Wow! First of all, I am so incredibly thankful for friends like Kim Ford, and so many countless others who held our arms up as we walked through this time. It has been just over two years now since Luke's relocation to Heaven, and I still have friends that reach out to me occasionally to let me know their hearts and prayers are with me, that the Lord has laid me on their hearts, and they continue to take us before the Father. I am so thankful for friendships, relationships, for others that challenge us to become the best version of ourselves we can be. Proverbs 27:17 says, "Iron sharpens iron; so a man sharpens the countenance of his friend." I encourage you if you do not have these types of friendships to seek them out, to pursue and intentionally choose to spend your time and have friendships with others who will draw you closer to the Father. Others who will challenge you in your thinking, who will show you how to love as Jesus loves. At different times in my life, I have prayed for these types of friendships. He always hears our prayers, and He will answer.

I remember my mom telling me a story about when she was a young mom, and new in her relationship with Jesus, that she cried out to the Lord for a mentor. Seemingly no one came into her life to fulfill that role. Decades later, she made a new and precious friend, Shirley Staires, mother of one of my closest friends, Sally Mulready. Shirley had written a book on being a godly wife and mother. She had written many principles in her book about making a house a home, about what it looks like for a wife to submit to her husband as the Lord asks us to in the Word.

As I read through her book, I exclaimed how everything in her book I had learned from my mom in growing up. We later learned Shirley had prayed the same prayer as my mom had, asking the Lord for a mentor. She too, felt like no one had come alongside her. The realization dawned on both of them how the Lord, indeed, had answered their prayers. The Holy Spirit Himself had come alongside them both and taught, trained, and mentored them. They had the same mentor. The Lord does not always answer us just as we think He should, but He is faithful, and He does answer.

I have learned how important it is to be intentional in our thought life. If we are not, we can open the door to the enemy, Satan, and allow him into our thoughts. In doing that, we give the devil a foothold. We have all experienced that path. One dark thought leads to another, and before we know it, we are consumed with fear, anxiety, or depression. That is not of God. Philippians 4:8 is one of my lifetime verses. 'For the rest, brethren, whatever is true, whatever is worthy of reverence and is honorable and seemly, whatever is just, whatever is pure, whatever is lovely and lovable, whatever is kind and winsome and gracious, if there is any virtue and excellence, if there is anything worthy of praise, think on and weigh and take account of these things (fix your mind on them). First of all, that is a lot of 'whatever's.' I think Paul is trying to get our attention with all that. I have used this verse to reprogram my mind, my thinking. I have had to choose to put my focus on what is true, what is good, what is pure, what is just. Is that how you think? I don't know about you, but it does not come naturally for me. THINK on these things. Is that a command? Think on these things. Not, "you might want to try to focus on the good..." THINK on these things. That is where we park our thoughts. It slams the door on the enemy trying to fill our mind with dark thoughts. It will change your life. It will allow you to live life to the fullest.

Another one of my lifetime verses I have chosen to keep as my focus is Isaiah 26:3. "You will keep him in perfect peace whose mind is stayed on You because he trusts in You." (ESV) I have found if I am intentional about keeping my thoughts and my focus on Him, rather than all the other concerns that could occupy my thoughts, He fills me with His peace. I choose to trust Him. I trust Him with my life. I trust Him that none of this is a surprise to Him and that He is there to walk with me, to journey with me to wholeness.

We very much choose where to park our thoughts. I choose not to dwell on the circumstances of Luke's last few minutes in this life. Instead, I focus on the good. More often than anything, when I picture him in my mind, I see him walking up to me in Heaven with his arms outstretched, his soul-warming smile touching me to my core. I see him thriving in Heaven in every way. He is loving children and others. I picture him with the two daughters I miscarried. I see him with my sister, my dad. He is laughing, witty, and a joy to everyone. He is using his gifts and talents. He is more content, happier, and fulfilled than he ever was on earth. He is whole. He never deals with temptation of any kind, because he no longer has to battle with the enemy of our souls. He plays guitar better than he did here and sings his

> We very much choose where to park our thoughts.

heart out. I know he will show me all around Heaven when I get there.

After my sister Alli died, my mom found a book *Within Heaven's Gates* by Rebecca Springer. I read it to my family after Luke went to be with Jesus. She talks all about Heaven and what it is like. She talks about lakes in Heaven. She says how tranquil they are, and that they are mostly used for transportation purposes – for someone to get from one place to another. As I read, I thought, "Oh, Luke will change that. He is wakeboarding, doing tricks, 360's, and stunts behind a boat." I read something about snow on the ground at some point in Heaven. I thought, "Oh good! Luke can snowboard!" I know he is doing what he loved best to do here on earth. Myself, as well as anyone else who knew him, would find great comfort in that.

We chose where we put our focus. We can choose to trust and walk in peace and joy, or we can allow our thoughts to take us down dark paths that can overwhelm and consume us. We can be in the midst of the most arduous journey, trying circumstances, the loss of a loved one, terrible health diagnosis and still choose to trust. A year after Luke died, I wrote in my journal, "Jesus, thank you for Your joy. I do want to live with great joy. Joy because You are within me and walk beside me. Joy in knowing I will be with all of these I love for eternity. I want to joy in the family before me."

I have come to realize how important it is to live in the moment. After my younger sister Alli died, my mom put a picture in her bedroom of Alli. She had an entire little area that seemed like a shrine to Alli. I remember thinking, "Mom, I am still here!" When we live distracted and thinking ahead, or dealing with the past, we miss the moment. It is the moments of our lives that give life meaning. My husband Greg is one of the best people I know at living in the moment. I will be lost in my thoughts, and then jarred back to the moment overhearing he and Joy teasing one another, playing silly games they make up, and just relishing the moment. It helps me choose to live in the moment as well. I find I have to be intentional about living in the moment, or I am not. Though I have lost my oldest son, and will no longer see him on this earth, I have a very real husband and five precious children that are still here. I don't want to miss a moment!!

My beautiful mother that wrote the poem has been widowed for twenty-three years since she was fifty-four. It was last August when she was diagnosed with advanced breast cancer, stage III C. The two 'words' to walk this difficult, all-consuming journey: 1. Take one day at a time, and 2. Look for the good – thank Him in everything, have sustained her. My sister and I have taken her to every appointment so that she would not be alone to walk this. Recently, she received trying news that was quite a blow to her, on several different fronts. She will have to go through thirty-three radiation treatments, Monday through Friday for six and a half weeks. The radiologist told her she would probably be doing an additional six months of chemotherapy after her surgery when she thought she would finish chemo in six weeks. Six additional months of chemo ravaging through her body when she thought she would be finished by then.

A friend of my sister's, Sandy McKinney, is a marathoner, that has qualified for the Boston marathon. She sent a text to my sister, comparing her recent run of the marathon to what Mom is facing. In her words, "When I ran the marathon on January 1st this year, my running partner said many things.

At one point he said, 'we've been running an hour and 53 minutes.' I responded saying, 'Please don't say it that way. It's too much! Too big! My brain starts to say I'll never make it!' (Because I wasn't even at the halfway mark at 1:53!!!) So - we decided we'd ONLY talk about the mile we were in! If that got to be too much, we were going to break it down to ½ miles, ¼ miles or even steps.

When we had been running (9:15 pace) for 3 hours and 55 minutes, he said, 'it's now been 3:55—it's your LAST FREAK-ING MILE!', I began to feel the joy that was 'coming in the morning.' It was the ending to more than 3,000 miles that I've run over the last three running seasons.

If you had told me how many miles would be required of me at the beginning, I would have said, "There's NO WAY I can, and there's NO WAY I will...'

Only think about the mile you're in. Day by day. Appointment by appointment. God will get you to the finish line. He always does."

Such timely advice for my mom. It applies to all of life. Just as the Lord told Mom to take it one day at a time, or for Sandy about the mile she was in, or the moment you are in right now; sometimes that is all we can take on. It is a protective, survival mode that we go into in our most challenging times, where it sometimes takes everything we have to maintain, to trust the Father in the present moment. When we choose to trust Him, He gives us peace. A peace that passes all understanding.

We choose where to park our thoughts. We choose where to dwell. We can allow ourselves to become totally overwhelmed, or we can choose to walk in peace. We have to be intentional in our thought life and not allow our emotions to get the best of us. I know I can only do this with Jesus, but with Him, I can do it. I can do all things through Christ who strengthens me.

I woke up this morning with another vivid dream. I asked the Lord to show me what it meant. In the dream, I unintentionally committed an offense against someone. When I found I had offended her, my initial reaction was to avoid her. Then I realized I needed to make it right. I needed to go to her, apologize outright, and in this case, take her a gift. Life is too short to carry grudges and offenses, whether you are on the offending end or the receiving end.

Sometimes when a loved one dies, we have unfinished business with them or regrets. Luke and Jace were very close growing up. They spent their entire lives together, even went through college together. When Luke could shirk responsibility, he would. He let Jace shoulder a lot through the years. Jace is very sensitive, and wanted to keep peace in the home so he was the one that often would step up and do things my husband was asking the boys to do. When Greg would say, "I need someone to do such and such…" it would get painfully quiet, no one would volunteer, and right at that well-timed second before Greg would get irritated that no one was willing to help him, Jace would speak up and say, "I will do it." Luke got away with too much as a result of that.

Jace began resenting Luke after a lifetime of this and let it drive a wedge between them. All of their lives they were together, including college classes. They did their senior paper together, in another class they were in the same group and did their senior project together. Yet they allowed the closeness to slip away because of the resentment. After Luke died, Jace lamented, "So much of that could have been resolved with just a single conversation!!" So much lost that could have been.

In Jace's situation, it was seemingly too late. It is never too late. I encouraged him to write Luke a letter in his journal. Have it out with him. Let Luke know how he offended him, how he resented it, and how it affected him. I encouraged him to tell Luke he forgave him, and even ask Luke's forgiveness for carrying that instead of confronting it and letting it come between them. I told him to deal through every aspect of this he could think of, and then to say, "Luke, I love you, I forgive you, but now I am allowing myself to let this go so that I do not have to live out the rest of my life dealing with guilt and remorse. I let this go, and we will have a two-sided conversation about this when I get to Heaven with you. In the meantime, I free myself to live life and live it to the fullest!"

Jace and I both learned a life lesson from this. We learned the importance of facing things. Deal through issues rather than letting them fester. Confront when necessary. Say what needs to be said. It also made me realize how often we think things in our heart about another person, and we hold back and don't share those things. Tell them they are beautiful, that their eyes are shining, how much their love and warmth comforts you, or all those sweet thoughts that come to mind. After Luke's funeral service, his best friend Chris said to me, "Why don't we say all these nice things about someone when we can? Why do we wait till it is too late?"

When it is appropriate, open the door of communication or conversation with others. When you notice hurt in their eyes, softly tell them what you see there, and if they are willing, let them share their story. I remember years ago seeing a young man in public whose clothes and style of dress screamed open rebellion. I prayed for him, but I have often thought I wish I would have just walked up and told him I could see that someone has hurt him, offended him deep down and opened a conversation that could have led to sharing with him what Jesus could do for his heart and life. Life is short. Say the things that need to be said. It may be exactly what they need to hear and you are the one that could say it.

Many people struggle for years over harsh words that were said between them and their loved one that were the last words they ever got to say to them. They didn't get to tell them they loved them. We cannot carry these regrets through the remainder of our lives. We have to let go of the "if only's."

We were at breakfast around our kitchen table the morning we heard about Luke's death. The thought came to my mind about his cousin, who was with him in consuming edibles. I picked up the phone, and the first words out of my mouth were, "Caleb, you have to let go of the 'if only's'. Caleb started crying. From the beginning, we chose forgiveness. We chose to forgive Caleb for any part he had in sharing in the experience with Luke. Luke made his own choices, but as for our part, we knew we needed to forgive.

My sister Toni shared with me a quote once, "Unforgiveness is like drinking poison and thinking it is going to harm the other person." Jesus forgave us, and He tells us to forgive. In *Life After Death*, Tony Cooke said, "When you forgive another person, the person you are really liberating is yourself." We knew that to release Caleb to become the man God wants him to be, that we needed to not carry resentment or unforgiveness toward him. Also, for our own sake, our relationship with the Lord, we did not want unforgiveness to stand in the way. Sin separates us from God. To have unforgiveness toward another is a sin. We want our relationship with the Father to be right, so we chose to forgive.

I have come to realize how important it is not to carry emotional baggage. I have known people carry hurts and offenses for decades. We cannot fool our bodies. Our bodies respond by breaking down physically. Cancer, disease, and illness result. The Word says, "A merry heart doeth good like a medicine, but a broken spirit dries the bones." Bitterness, unforgiveness, resentment, hostility, and hatred will affect a person physically. It is not worth it. On the other hand, it is SO worth it to face an offense, have a conversation to free both yourself and the other person.

Being intentional in your thought life means taking a good look within. Ask the Holy Spirit to reveal to you anything that is unresolved in your heart and life. Then go and resolve it. Let the Holy Spirit pour His healing balm over you. Whether the other person responds the way you think they should or not, do it for your well-being, your wholeness, your health. You are worth it! Then you will find you no longer need to dwell on things mentally and emotionally that have a negative impact on you. You can begin to choose to walk in joy and peace. It is a beautiful way to live.

TAKING CARE OF YOU

Let gratitude be your source of joy.

Let trust be your source of peace.

Let encouragement be your source of strength.

Let Love be your source of life.

Spoken by Rob Koke at his son's wedding

W hen my younger sister Alli died, I did not know the first thing about how to intentionally walk through the grief of her loss for me to become whole again. I had moved from my home in Kingwood, Texas where I grew up and had gone off to college at Oral Roberts University five years before, to go through a four-year nursing program. I then stayed in Tulsa, and worked as a nurse for a year upon graduating. I went on a missions trip where I was helping to lead a team and was over the females on the trip. I came back home as my sister was dying, literally left the mission field in Guatemala, went straight to her bedside, and spent her last seventeen days with her there. As I had mentioned, I had zero support system in Houston. I had uprooted from everyone and everything to return home to be with my sister and my family.

Because I did not know how to deal with her loss, I didn't. I suppressed my grief and went on living. I was in seven car accidents within a year and a half of her death, five where the cars were totaled. As an adult, I have since read that car accidents are often a result of suppressed grief. I did not know how important it was to simply cry when I needed to cry, to allow myself to grieve when my heart was aching. I did not realize that tears came more easily early on, and it was important not to bottle those up. I did not know then that when we suppress our hurts and our feelings, our physical body carries the weight of our loss, and we begin having physical and health issues. Unresolved grief shows up in physical problems in our body. I have lived all of my adult life in neck and back pain as a result of all the car wrecks, and have dealt with terrible migraine headaches that had gotten to where I had them four and five days a week. I have lived in pain. Thankfully this past year I found a product that has changed my life. It is natural, no side effects, wild harvested organic nutrition that has been an absolute game changer for me. I have not had a migraine in months, and I feel better inside of me than I have in decades. Our bodies are wired for food, healed through nutrition, and if we are smart enough to put the right nutrients in them, they can do what our Creator created them to do, and heal themselves.

After losing Luke, I became very intentional about dealing

with the grief of his loss, as I have mentioned so that my children and husband and I would be able to become healthy and whole again. The grief of his loss has still taken a toll on my physical body. I have had several episodes of incredible incapacitating pain, where I felt as if I had a heart attack. Several times I passed out in pain with the most recent time being while I was driving. I ended up in the hospital. It was not my heart; my heart was not having any issues. I have since found out that grief and loss can radically deplete our bodies supply of calcium and magnesium. My body's stores of those were almost completely depleted. I have seen a naturopath doctor that is helping me resolve that. The way my body manifested that deficiency was in this intense cramping that felt like I had an elephant standing on my chest.

It is so important to know and realize that our body will be impacted by grief and loss so that we can take care of ourselves. Our diet is so important; we need to make healthy food choices to give our body what it requires us through this time. I mentioned before that I had massages monthly for the first year. I know that did so much for my overall health. I know it did so much for me physically and emotionally as well. I am preaching to the choir here as I mention the importance of slowing life down, and paying attention to what our body is telling us to maintain our health. This allows our body and soul time to grieve our loss.

Anyone that is a caretaker for their loved one needs to be aware of the toil that takes on their own body, and the importance of taking care of themselves. When we are on an airplane, and they are giving the safety spiel, they always say to put on your mask before you put one on your children. If you pass out for lack of oxygen, what good are you in helping your children survive? You have to take care of you and find ways to nurture yourself to be able to nurture those around you. If you allow yourself to become completely rundown, then who is going to take care of the others? It is not selfish to take care of yourself; you have to, to take care of anyone else you love.

Find the ways that work for you to take care of you. It may be relaxing baths with a few drops of lavender essential oil added to the bath with candlelight and relaxing music. It may be long walks. It may be alone time. Journal time. Massages. Taking time to sit beside the lake and reflect, contemplate, think, and heal. It may be long hikes, time spent in sharing with friends. It may be going to a great movie. Laugh. Laugh with your spouse. Smile. Smile at your spouse. Cry. Cry with your spouse, or someone safe. Watch a sunset. Find things that move your soul. Sit and watch your children play and just delight in them. Delight in a child's laugh. Marvel in the beauty and uninhibitedness of a child. Sing. Listen to uplifting music. See the beauty in your world. Marvel at Creation. Allow yourself to feel. Let emotion out so that it is not locked inside you. Whatever this looks like for you; it is critical that you take care of you.

I previously mentioned that exercise is also such an important piece of the puzzle. It is one of the healthiest ways I know to relieve stress. Swim. Play racquetball, tennis, pickleball. Go for a walk, a jog, or a good long hike in nature. Lift weights. Go rollerblading, play volleyball, soccer. Do something athletic with friends. Make love with your spouse. Exercise and lovemaking release endorphins in our body that bring healing. Exercise makes us feel better about ourselves, our physical appearance. It increases our stamina. It helps with stress management.

Since I was sixteen, I have made exercise a part of my life. I don't just exercise in spurts. It is part of my lifestyle. When I started having babies and was unable to go to the gym, I went to a used sports store and bought a stair stepper. I bought weights to use from home. I make exercise part of my daily routine. I wake up each morning, thank the Lord for each new day, this gift of life. I start with my thankful journal, thanking Him for three to ten or twelve things He did for me in the day before. I thank Him for the hard things as well. I spend time worshipping Him, praying and in reading the Word, my Bible. It is my manna each day; it gives me what I need to get me through the day, not just to survive, but to thrive. I take the time to still myself before my Abba, Father and to listen to Him, even if it is just for two to three minutes. It grounds me. Then I exercise. I often double task and stair step while I read my Bible and then a chapter from a personal development book, or devotional.

Years ago, my sister, Toni Fowler, wrote an article called "Thriving as a Wife and a Mother." I am so proud of my sister! She truly lives this. She is a gift, and it is an honor to do this journey of life with her. She recently published a book on this very theme. She has been such a remarkable blessing to go to when I am in need of parenting wisdom. I am so grateful I have been able to bounce thoughts off of her through the years. Her book, *Thrive*, co-authored with her husband David, may be the best book on parenting out there, as well as teaching you to live with your heart, and learning to thrive in every area of your life. Her book is chock full of pearls of wisdom and principles to live your life by. It is life challenging, as well as life-changing.

She is the mother of ten children and has such wisdom on parenting your children even into the adult years. We never really stop parenting, our role as parents changes into a deepening friendship with our adult children. We consider ourselves blessed when our adult kids come to us for counsel. I want to share with you here the article she wrote years ago.

Thriving as a Wife and a Mother

Is it possible to thrive, even in your heart and soul, as a mother and wife in today's times? Emphatically, Yes! If we maintain certain attitudes and remember some basics.

Every day, at least once, someone asks me, "How do you do it?" I presume that means 'how do you maintain sanity, much less peace, and joy, with your load?' I have ten children, homeschool them and manage a ministry of hospitality out of our home. And I love life! Not because I am "Susie-homemaker," but because my Heavenly Father has imparted to me some basics of thriving.

When asked the question, "How do you do it?", I have always responded:

1. "It is the grace of God."
2. "The joy of the Lord is my strength!"

Well, recently I realized these two factors make me 90% of whom I am. But there is a third dimension, and that is what I've learned to do to take care of myself and the nurturing of my well-being.

Regressing momentarily, I must elaborate on the first two points since that is what primarily enables me to excel beyond my limitations.

Number 1: Never take for granted the grace of God in your life. One of my favorite scriptures is: "In our weakness, Christ's strength will be perfected!" (2 Cor. 12:9)

Rather than be threatened or limited by my own weakness, I have learned to fully embrace my weaknesses and admit them to my Father - acknowledging my limitations, looking to Him immediately to "come through" with His strength.

Such as when I run out of peace and patience, and the day is far from over I simply say, "Lord, this is it. This is all I've got, and as far as I can go. You must take over in me and give me that love that You have commanded me to walk in!" And then, like Superman swooping down with a blanket of love, peace, or patience – He faithfully comes through! Because He

221

thrives on proving to you His perfect strength in your weakness. On a scale of 1—10, you and God together are a 10! On the days that you are only a 2, He will be an 8 for you, if you let Him! And when you are a 9, He will still come through for that last little bit that you need, if you only call on Him—He is so good!

The second most important ingredient to inner success is joy. For when you have joy, all of life seems good. And when you don't, everything is a burden. You know what I am talking about, don't you?

The Bible says, "The joy of the Lord is your strength." When you lose your joy, you literally lose the strength you need to perform the basics.

The greatest way I know to maintain joy is through a grateful heart. Singing helps me — I constantly sing when I am not conversing, especially praise and worship songs, which continually remind me of the greatness of our God and feed one's spirit.

You have heard it so often now it seems almost trite, but it's so key.... Always be ever mindful of how truly blessed you are. Focus consciously on all the little and big ways that you are so blessed. Learn to delight yourself in your children, rather than always letting them 'zap' your energy.

Watch them and look for the special, precious, unique ways about each one and let that delight you and literally fill your soul with joy.

During my last pregnancy, as with most of them, I was so exhausted all the time that I could barely get off the couch. Instead of feeling guilty about it, I decided I would 1.) let my children step up to new levels of responsibility—which is only beneficial, and 2.) I would simply lay there and really watch them, and truly delight and feed my soul on all their sweet little ways that I do not take time to notice when I'm being so efficient and productive.

And now for my third piece of the pie. I have learned how critical it is to take care of myself, nurturing myself, even occasional pampering if you will.

Let me explain. I have always believed that in laying down your life, you will truly find it. Our greatest joys truly come in serving others. But to do that, we must love our husbands and our children, or whomever God has placed in our lives, so much that we refuse to allow ourselves to remain a worn out, whipped rag – just for their benefit.

I say remain because we all struggle with the perils of exhaustion quite regularly. Don't be discouraged by that – it is par for the territory of motherhood.

But we must do what it takes to REFILL our cups continually. Women tend to get the idea that it is most noble to spend one's self until there is nothing left.

Well, that self-sacrifice is good if we are only running a sprint. But if we are in for the long haul, we must learn how to replenish ourselves. To be what those dependent on us need, we must work to maintain a "full cup" in ourselves.

We all know the obvious things, granted that is hard enough to do. Time connecting with the Lord, plenty of sleep, exercise, better nutrition, etc., but what about those things that feed our soul, refresh us and perk us up — just making us feel better overall and enabling us to like our life and all that it presents to us.

It is so important to have fun together as a family — special trips, family nights or even just sitting around the kitchen talking and laughing together.

I also highly recommend a trip alone, every six months or so to a local hotel or B & B. One or two days away to sleep, read, pray, and regroup will make you a completely new woman. You will come home so refreshed and ready to be all you need to be for your family again.

Some of you may struggle with the next part as too "old-fashioned," but it is an issue that must be addressed. I have seen marriages break up over this one. Your husband should always be treasured as your 'biggest baby' of all!

The children will come and go, but hopefully, he is there forever. Talk about nurturing him for the long haul! Never neglect to nurture him. You must always remember that he matters more than all the other activities that you do.

1 Cor. 7:11 tells us that man was created for the glory of God, but woman was created for the glory of man (pretty heavy truth, ladies). Proverbs 31:12 says, "She will comfort, encourage, and do him only good all the days of her life." Tall order! I'm still working hard on that one.

Almost nothing will feed your soul as much as a thriving relationship with your husband. And I must tell you, one of the biggest inhibitors to that is a critical perspective toward him.

He will never be the best of all your best friends' husbands put together. You may have struggled with how little you have managed to change him, since marrying him.

The truth is, that's not really your job. Your job is to love him. There is such a security and satisfaction when you choose to accept each other just the way you are — for better or for worse — extremely imperfect.

And by you choosing to do that you will find it cultivates the spirit of unconditional love in your marriage and it works both ways. And now for some very practical ideas to stimulate your own thinking on things you can do for yourself.

Massages are wonderful and are a regular part of our family's health maintenance. As good as massages feel, they are equally as good for you. They have tremendous physical and emotional benefits.

Chiropractic care can do wonders to "straighten things up" that cause more problems than you may realize. Crooked spines are big-time responsible for the majority of headaches, backaches, and other tensions that you put up with daily.

Facials, manicures, pedicures, and new hairstyles can all give one a major lift. Clothes of natural fibers can make one feel so comfortable. Every season you should have a couple of garments that feel so good they comfort your soul just to slip into.

Long phone calls to your best friends, after the kids are down, across the globe or even across town can do wonders.

Speaking of the children, do them a favor and put them to bed at a decent time, so that they are properly rested, which makes for happier, healthier children and parents.

After they go to bed you should have an hour to yourself to do what you need to do — mail, phone calls, then a much-needed bubble bath a few times a week!

If you add 2 cups of pure apple cider vinegar to a hot bath and soak about 20 minutes, it will chemically take the toxins from your body that cause physical aches and pains.

Your body will not retain the odor of the cider vinegar. You don't even have to rinse it off, and by the way, it will cause your skin to be extra silky.

The achy exhaustion we are all too familiar with at the day's end drains with the bath water, and you simply feel sleepy. And you will sleep well! Add bubbles and a candle or two and maybe even a glass of wine. One or two glasses a week will do almost everybody good.

And then when you get into bed, you should have a "comfort drawer" next to your bed — filled with the sweet things that minister to your soul when you even open it.

Candles, cards, a few chocolates, aromatic sachets, special souvenirs from a treasured memory, little love gifts made by your children, a love note from your husband.

Open it and indulge yourself as you read your Bible, poetry, or anything inspirational that puts your heart in the right places.

Another fun thing for your soul can be decorating. Occasionally, pick up little things, or even bigger things as money allows, that add sweet touches to your home. You will find that they give the whole family a lift.

Oh, and never forget to lavishly enjoy life's free(est) gifts: the sunsets or sunrises, depending on your lifestyle, flowers, birds singing, walks in the parks, music, children's laughter or cuddling a baby. Allow these moments to wash over you at every opportunity, literally permeating your body with peace and joy that feeds health and life to your body.

One more practical tip along these lines — is deep breathing exercises as you are going to sleep. As you lie on your pillow at night, right before you go to sleep, take about 10 of the deepest breaths your body can handle.

As you exhale — consciously let go of stress, anger, resentment, disappointment and hurt. As you inhale — breathe in Jesus, joy, peace, love, and forgiveness. You choose each day what needs to go out and what needs to come into your being. That way all that unhealthy residue of the day does not lock up in your body to do its damage as you sleep.

I am not encouraging you to simply indulge yourself, for indulgence sake. But to think about little and big things, low budget or no budget things, that feed your soul and make it fuller, so that you may have more to give those you love.

The fuller that You are, the more the Lord can use you for His purposes.

And now, I want to share my final and biggest way of maintaining my sanity and wholeness. And this is just to those of you who are married. It is not love making—though that is another, yes indeed.

But it is the hour I spend at the end of my day re-grouping with my husband. It falls around midnight for us, and we do this at least six days a week, even when he is on the road we talk on the phone.

Get on the same wavelength with each other about every significant thing in each other's heart and day. This isn't a dump session, though unfortunately, it must sometimes be. But it is sharing our hearts and mind. We talk about who we each talked to that day. The children, homeschooling, the job, dreams, visions, ideas, politics, Rush Limbaugh, philosophy, theology, new developing understandings of God and life itself, far out thoughts, and all that we are.

Because then, in coming face to face with who we really are—for better or for worse—and who our spouse is, together we present it all to Father God to do with as He wishes, and as only He can.

Not fighting or resisting reality, but fully embracing our authentic selves, which always brings freedom and richness.

You must choose to embrace life and every inch of it as fully and positively as you can, that you might live it as richly and truly as God intended for you to live it!

TONI FOWLER, COPYRIGHT 1998

My sister Toni sent me a text recently that is along this same thought of how to thrive. "Every moment becomes more sacred when you choose love over snippety or indifference. And you must choose it. It is up to us to diligently guard the condition of our own heart and keep it soft and pliable toward the Father and others. For our very health and well-being depends on it!" As I previously touched on, she has taught me her life practice of taking time each day, two to three times a day, for at least two to three minutes, to still myself before the Father and know that He is God. When you wake up, before even getting out of bed is an excellent time to do this. If you take the time for a nap later in the day is another good time, and finally, when you get into bed at night, before falling off to sleep are moments that can be taken to do this.

Take the time then to listen to your own heart, soul, and body. Is anything wrong, or off-kilter, something not settling right, or robbing you of your peace? Put it before the Father until He brings you to a place of peace over it. Commit it to Him.

You may want to listen to relaxing sounds, like the waves of the ocean, and then, as she talked about in her article, take slow deep breaths, breathe in His presence, His goodness, His love. Let it wash over you as you inhale. As you exhale, breathe out any angst, turmoil, or disease process and let that go. The Lord says in Psalms 37:6 to, "Commit your way to the Lord—roll and repose (each care of) your load on Him; trust also in Him, and He will bring it to pass." As you are able to roll your cares and concerns over to Him, He gives you peace. This will ground you.

Ask Him to show you if there are any areas that you need to be aware of, anything He wants to address. And then listen. Learn to know and hear His voice. He is always speaking if we will quiet ourselves to listen. He says in John 10:27, "The sheep that are My own hear and are listening to My voice, and I know them and they follow Me." Allow the Holy Spirit within you to

> He is always speaking if we will quiet ourselves to listen.

guide you, to show you what He wants to reveal to you each day.

Along with this same idea of taking care of you, and my sister's article on thriving, I want to share a letter I wrote my nephew in response to a comment he made one evening when we were with him. I will give him a different name in the letter to protect his identity. To me, this topic, about marriage, is a huge part of taking care of you. For those married, or thinking of marriage one day, it greatly affects your well-being.

∽

Chase,

Last night you made a comment about "picking the right one." Having been married for 25 years to the same wonderful man and having six wonderful kids to show for it, I have a couple of thoughts I want to share.

"Picking the right one" is a part of it. Even looking in the right places to find her as your grandfather suggested last night—recommending finding a great church with a strong singles group. Dear friends of ours pastor Shoreline in Austin, with a congregation of about 5,000. That might be a great place to start.

Like anything in life—there are daily choices we all make. What we choose to believe and dwell on in our hearts and thoughts will make a huge impact on our lives.

Intentionally choosing to have a thankful, grateful heart is a huge key to a successful marriage. Being intentional about time spent together—dating one another, playing together, laughing, loving, great and frequent love-making. When we date regularly, we don't discuss kids, we have fun and enjoy one another's company.

Greg and I have had our marriage issues. Every marriage does. Every marriage involves two imperfect people. We choose to work through problems. We have decided each other is worth it, so we work through things together.

Keeping the Lord central in a marriage is huge, as is praying together regularly. We take issues before the Lord and ask for His wisdom. He always meets us. Truly the marriage that prays together stays together. So does the marriage that plays together stay together. Why not both?

After 25 years, my heart still leaps when Greg walks into a room. It takes two to make a marriage great, but there are seasons in marriage. My dad once told me, "Some say marriage is 50–50. It is really 90–10. Each side giving ninety." He also said, "You marry a family." I had no idea how true that was until I thankfully married into the tremendous family I did. I have known many others that have struggled extensively because of the family they married into.

It is so incredibly worth it!! Having someone you not only love, but like, to go through life with—to share both the joys and struggles of life together—from living life, to parenting, to sharing sunsets, the Lord's great outdoors, laughter, adventure, doing life with your best friend, to sitting on a porch swing together in old age—like your grandparents after 62 years. They have shared a lifetime of memories. When we celebrated our 25th, we shared with each other years of memories - the good, the bad, and the ugly—but we have had so many great memories.

We are so richly blessed. We have had the Lord's blessing on our lives and marriage. It has enabled us to weather the storms—like Luke's death. That has been the hardest thing we have ever had to walk through together, but even in it, we have seen the Lord's goodness.

We try to focus on one another's strengths, rather than our weaknesses. With Luke's death, we have had to come to a whole new level of learning to cling to the Lord – we have done it together.

Choices. We make them every day. Every minute. Learning to take "every thought captive to the obedience of Christ."

"Finally brethren, whatever is true, whatever is noble, right, pure, lovely, whatever is admirable—if anything is excellent or praiseworthy—think on these things." (NIV) We have learned to look for the good in one another, and to focus on that.

Chase, I don't know where you are in your relationship with the Lord. I am pretty sure you asked Him into your heart when you were younger. I encourage you to rededicate your life to Him. Ask Him to come into your heart, be Lord of your life. We are all created by our Creator with such a need for Him; a void that only He can fill.

He wants to bring you to a place of wholeness, that you won't find anywhere outside of Him. We can run to Him every time we fall down, fall short, and lay it all before His feet, and let Him work restoration in our hearts and lives.

My last thought on what makes a good marriage is the importance of forgiveness. There have been times when I went to Greg and asked his forgiveness for wronging him when I didn't feel like I was the one in the wrong. There usually was an attitude or something there where I was in the wrong, but I found as I humbled myself and asked his forgiveness it led to the restoration of our relationship.

We have decided we want to grow old together. It is a decision. A decision based on a commitment we made to one another years ago when we said, "I do."

My dad once said, "Your mom is not the same woman I married. But then again, I am not the same man she married. You have to choose to grow together." We choose, we make the decision to grow together. We choose to learn from our mistakes. We choose to find common interests that allow us to be one another's recreational playmate so we can spend time together doing fun things we enjoy together. We make our decisions; we make our choices. With God's help, we make good ones.

As you choose to rededicate your life to Jesus, I encourage you to read His word. I think of how many lives have been lost over the centuries for us to have His word, and realize how vital it is to our lives. "Thy word is a lamp unto my feet, and a light unto my path." I can always turn to His word and find the wisdom and guidance I need to live life. A great place to start is in some of Paul's letters – Ephesians, Philippians, Colossians. Also, the gospels – Matthew, Mark, Luke (my favorite), and John where you hear His words, His heart.

I said all that to say this; there is much more to a great marriage than simply picking the right one. Like a garden that needs to be tended and nurtured that will one-day yield beauty, a marriage also needs to be tended and nurtured. The best gift you will give your children one day is to love their momma.

Love you, Kim

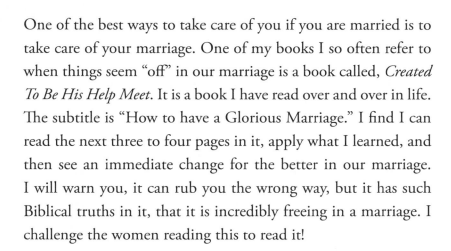

One of the best ways to take care of you if you are married is to take care of your marriage. One of my books I so often refer to when things seem "off" in our marriage is a book called, *Created To Be His Help Meet*. It is a book I have read over and over in life. The subtitle is "How to have a Glorious Marriage." I find I can read the next three to four pages in it, apply what I learned, and then see an immediate change for the better in our marriage. I will warn you, it can rub you the wrong way, but it has such Biblical truths in it, that it is incredibly freeing in a marriage. I challenge the women reading this to read it!

DEEP INNER HEALING

"What we have once enjoyed and deeply loved we can never
lose, for all that we love deeply becomes a part of us."

Helen Keller

A
t one year after Luke went to be with Jesus, I was still
struggling with lack of motivation. At the same time, I
was standing in awe of Jesus and what He was doing in
each of our hearts. He was bringing about a deep inner work—
inspired of God.

I want to share with you how I have experienced profound
healing in my heart and life. There is a healing work that only
the Holy Spirit can do in our hearts and lives. I have had several
epiphany experiences where the Holy Spirit has done deep inner
healing within me. One of these times happened when our entire family of eight was camping at Lake Tenkiller in Oklahoma
for the week. I woke up about four in the morning after having a recurring dream I often had. I called it my, "disorganized
dream." I had had it in hundreds of different scenarios it seemed.

One example was that our family was about to leave for a flight to Germany together (which we have not done). I was attempting to pack my suitcase and could not find the things I needed to make complete outfits—the leggings for this outfit, the shoes for that one… I was tearing up my closet as the deadline to leave was quickly approaching. I could not get it all together. Greg was telling me it was time to go. The more frustrated he got with me, the less I got done. Finally, he would walk out with the rest of the family, and they would leave without me so that they would not miss the flight. I would have missed out on the trip because I was so completely disorganized. In these dreams, it was always different scenarios, but each time I was ridiculously disorganized.

There is a healing work that only the Holy Spirit can do in our hearts and lives.

In life, I would not say I am highly organized, but I do spin a lot of plates and get an incredible amount done. I don't fear not being able to get it all done. I mentioned we have had kettle corn weekends where we have three and four events going on simultaneously. I am the one that pulls together all the details to make it happen smoothly. I line up the help. We may have events going on in different cities, several setups at an event. Every set up has a hundred different details that have to fall in place. My family will call me, incredulous if one set up is missing twisty ties for the bags, or a stirring spoon for the lemonade. They cannot believe I overlooked one detail.

I worked as an organ donor coordinator, coordinating events, making dozens of phone calls for each donation, organizing every aspect that has to fall in place for an organ donation to happen. We have taken motorhome trips where I am cooking, baking and packing food for 27 meals and cannot forget a single item for a meal because we won't have access to a store during that time. It makes me laugh when the family cannot fathom how I could forget the ketchup we need one time during the trip, they all expect me to have it all together.

So, why was I having these crazy disorganized dreams? It drove me crazy. I guess I am a slow learner. My sister told me recently that whenever she has a meaningful dream that she wakes up and remembers, she asks the Lord to show her what the meaning or significance of the dream was. Well, this morning at 4 am on the camping trip as I woke up with yet another disorganized dream, I cried out to the Lord, "What the heck is this about? Why do I keep having these dreams? What does it mean? What are you trying to show me?!!!!!"

I quietly slipped outside with my journal and my Bible since everyone was sleeping, stepping over masses of bodies to get out the door. I sat before the Lord and said, "I need to know what you are saying to me!!" He started speaking to me and I started journaling. He showed me three different areas I struggled with in my subconscious mind. He showed me that I struggled with a fear of rejection that I had since before birth. My mom always told me she was on birth control when she got pregnant with me and that I was an accident. She never once told me I was a miracle because, with the Lord, there are no accidents. He showed me how it played out in my heart and life. In all my dating relationships, I kept guys at arm's distance from my life, as well as my heart. I was afraid of being rejected, so I rejected them first before it could ever happen to me. He showed me thing after thing as I journaled page after page after page. I was crying, sobbing, as He continued gently working, healing my wounded heart.

He showed me that I had a fear of being unloved. Growing up, my older sister Toni was an extremely outgoing, sanguine extrovert that knew everyone. Her friends ranged from her age to sixty years older and everywhere in between. That is more normal for adults, but rather unusual for someone in junior high. Everyone knew Toni. My younger sister Alli had an incurable disease—Cystic Fibrosis. The Lord used Alli's disease in our lives to bring us to Him. We walked a journey of having to learn to trust in Him. We went to a church of 3500 people. Dad was an elder and well known in the congregation. I often overheard adults in conversation, "The Swain's have another daughter?!" I was that quiet one in the middle, the one no one knew. My dad used to tell me he felt like he had to walk on eggshells around me to not hurt my feelings. So, I felt invisible and unloved. My younger sister, because of her illness, got a lot of attention, Toni got it because she was the squeaky wheel. I don't mean that in a negative light, it's just that she was much more verbal.

He showed me the third fear I was dealing with was a fear of abandonment. I had a wonderful family growing up. We were so blessed. My dad was a man of principle, and he was passionate about life, he loved and adored us all. One day he taught me to change a tire on the car. At the time, I worked at Red Lobster and wore a uniform to work with a very short skirt. About a week later I was coming home late from work. Actually, it was morning, 1:15 a.m. I had a flat. I was ten minutes from home, and still living at home, so I did what every high school girl does, and called her dad to come to help her. He showed up, was very irritated with me for calling him, and he stood there and made me change the tire-in my very short skirt! Some nice man stopped to help - looked at me, looked at my dad quizzically, and tentatively said, "Can I help you?" Before I could answer my dad said, "No, she's fine." The man had a look of concern and then drove away.

Afterward, my dad said, "Now, what did you learn from that lesson?" I angrily blurted out, "That I can't trust you!" He replied, "No, you learned that you could do that if you need to." Well, that may have been what he wanted me to learn, and honestly, I can see the value in that, but I did feel like he abandoned me that night when I needed him. It was dangerous for a young teenage woman to be changing a tire in a short skirt on a dark stretch of road at that time of night. So back to this night of camping at Lake Tenkiller, the Lord showed me how I had a fear of abandonment since then.

He later showed me how that went back farther than even me. My dad dealt with severe feelings of abandonment his entire life because his dad left him when he was a child. Unknowingly, his dad made numerous attempts to reach out to him, but his mom rejected those attempts, leaving him with a lifetime of feeling abandoned. It was a generational issue that was surfacing in my dream.

These three fears kept resurfacing in my dreams until I finally let the Holy Spirit work in me and show me how these fears had a hold on me. He kept opening my heart to truth and as I poured out my heart in my journal, He poured healing into my heart. I sat there and sobbed and sobbed to my core. And as I sobbed and released all this to Jesus, the Master Healer and Comforter brought such complete healing to my heart. I know, because after He and I dealt with all that, and I released hurt to Him, the dreams stopped. I no longer have those dreams. There was a time or two sometime later that I had that dream, and both times I went to the Lord and said, "OK, Father, am I still hanging onto something here?"

He took me down the path of forgiveness. My dad had already passed away, but I chose to forgive him. I have found that whenever I struggle with forgiving a difficult offense, I say, "Father, I forgive, but like the man in the Bible that said, 'Yes, Lord, I believe, but help my unbelief,' yes Lord, I forgive, but help me to forgive." To forgive is to let go. I did go to my mom and confront her about always telling me I was an accident, and how that had made such an impact on me. My mom is a wonderful woman of God, a woman of faith. She has always talked to us about our "confession" and how the words of our mouths matter. Ironically enough, when I confronted her, she sat there looking at me. She did not say, "I am so sorry! Will you please forgive me?" as I expected her to say. So, I found that even though she did not respond as I thought she should, I still had to choose to forgive her. That choosing to forgive her was part of what I needed for complete healing.

The sweet thing was that after the intense healing work the Holy Spirit took me through after I had journaled about twelve pages of insight He shed for me, after sobbing my eyes and heart out, it started raining. Gently at first. I grabbed up my Bible, journal, and headed back into the motorhome. Then it started pouring down rain. About that time, I was feeling completely free emotionally, and I felt washed, bathed in utter joy. I sensed such a complete release from all this that had been entangling me. I had been rejoicing as I ran for cover inside. The family was all beginning to wake up. It was evident to them I had just come through something very emotional. As the rain torrents came down, I felt the Father sharing tears of joy and overcoming with me. In my family's grogginess of just having awakened, I shared through choking, joyful sobs the release Jesus had given me. They celebrated with me. That is how our Father is. That showed me yet again, how genuinely He loves us.

I shared all of this in so much depth because I want you to see how the Holy Spirit can work in our hearts and lives if we let Him. I often ask Him to show me specific areas—maybe if there is anyone I have offended that I need to ask forgiveness or any number of areas. It is amazing how He works and brings things to our remembrance. Like my nephew, Daniel's poem talks about, the Lord wants us to be free. If we are whole, we can lead others to wholeness. Only the Holy Spirit can reveal these kinds of profound truths. He knows your history. He knows everything about you and what makes you tick, what weighs on your heart, and where the Lord wants to bring freedom to you.

Just as the Father wants to heal your brokenness, the enemy wants to keep you broken. He does not want you to be free. He wants to hold you captive. He will feed you lies to keep you in a position of feeling unworthy to be used to minister to others. He will remind you of every area in which you fall short.

You are a serious threat to the enemy when you walk in peace and joy and know who you are in the Father; when you know you are His sons and daughters. We have to learn to recognize the lies of the enemy and choose to walk in the Lord's truth instead. Take those lies from the enemy and throw them right back in his face. Let him know you are no longer buying into that. Then let the Father show you what He thinks of you. Jesus wants to heal your brokenness, so that he can turn around and use you in the lives of others to heal theirs.

If we allow it to, honestly wrestling with loss and journeying through grief can make us stronger and better. It can enable us to help others as they navigate through their grief. Sometimes only those that have walked through the same path can minister to others experiencing similar pain. The Lord continues to open doors when we are willing to be used by Him.

As we choose to walk in the Lord's truth and believe in His deep, incredible love for us, we become who He created us to be. Others will know we have been with Him by our love. You are the steward of your own heart. The Lord says to "Guard your heart with all vigilance and above all else that you guard, for out of it flows the springs of life." (Proverbs 4:23)

I have to admit, at this point, I had thought I was completely finished writing this book. I even had it into the editor, when last night I had not one, but two of the disorganized dreams. I haven't had one in the past two years. The Lord showed me this was not just for me this time, but to expound on it in my writing.

I have learned when I have a dream in the night, the importance of waking up and writing it down. I have had the Lord show me riveting thoughts and revelation during the night that I knew I would remember later, and yet, in the morning I would have zero recollection of what it was He spoke to me. Write your thoughts down as they are flowing from Him to you.

In the first dream last night, we made a surprise visit to see an aunt in Pennsylvania. She came to visit us recently for the first time in ten years, but we had not been there in longer than that. I was with a group that included my husband, and when we showed up at the door my aunt did not even seem surprised over our 'surprise' visit. I was aware that our time was extremely limited because we had another flight to catch and we were only dropping in to say hello. There were quite a few people inside. My grandmother (who passed away 40 years ago) was sitting near two other women. She seemed very self-conscious and glanced down at her shirt which I then realized was inside out. I asked, "Oh! Are y'all in the middle of a dressing change?" They indicated they were. I herded our entire group out to give them some privacy. When I stepped outside, I realized they were all gone. They had left without me to catch the flight. It was too late for them to come back to get me or they would miss the flight. I was struggling with why my husband Greg would have left without me, surely, he would have noticed I was not with them!

I woke up realizing this was from that deep-rooted fear of abandonment. Was he rejecting me in leaving me? Was there something I had done in our relationship that left me being unloved? This was all three of the fears that I thought I had previously fully dealt through with the Holy Spirit. My early morning thoughts drifted to my fifth son and I started praying for him. As I went to bed, I asked the Lord to give me answers as I slept. Instead of answers, I awakened two hours later having had the worst disorganized dream of my life.

In the second dream, my husband and I were at an extended motivational type event. I was up for an award. We had an assignment where we were to read something and do a write up about it. A woman was impressing to me the importance of this award and said, "I hope you don't mess this up. Well, you won't!" There were only four of us across the country that were being considered for the award. Greg and I had arrived early, and I stashed my things in a compartment in the room where we would be staying. Later, one of my neighbors arrived, threw my things out, and replaced them with his things. Each night for five nights we would be wearing business attire. I then realized I had forgotten to pack! I had no dresses to wear but only the shorts I was wearing. There was a Dillard's nearby, so I started looking for my purse that had been thrown out. I had several friends there close to my size and I was asking them if I could borrow a dress, and if they could wear it on a later night. They were looking at me doubtfully, when an acquaintance spoke up and said she brought something for me to wear that night.

Greg showed up with my accessories and purse. I ran back to look in all the compartments where we had placed our things to try to find my shoes. As I did, I almost plunged over a cliff. Dreams are crazy like that and do not always make sense in our natural minds. I woke up remembering every detail so vividly. I implored the Lord to show me why I again had this type of dream. He wasn't giving me what I had asked Him for and that was regarding some questions about my son.

He reminded me of the three fears He had addressed in these disorganized dreams: fear of rejection, fear of being unloved, and fear of abandonment. Now it was time to do some battle in the spirit realm. The first dream certainly had that—fear that if I am not good enough, if I don't love just right that my husband would leave me. I renounce that lie of the enemy and remove it from my very DNA. It went back to my dad's fear of abandonment because he was abandoned by his dad. I believe that in Heaven he and his dad and his mother have resolved that. He is now loved, and so am I.

I rebuke roots of self-hatred that came down through my other grandmother, the one that was in the dream. I break and renounce all thoughts, curses, and agreements I have made with the enemy over this. I remove it from my DNA forever in Jesus name!

I renounce the lies I have believed in my self-conscious about fear of rejection. I break the power of the enemy over my mind with these lies. I will no longer buy into them! I renounce them and throw off this weight that has entangled me. You love me! I break the fear of rejection and remove it from my DNA. I send these lies back to the pit of hell. They are no longer a part of me.

I am healed and delivered of the Lord. I am His child. I am a daughter of the Most High God! Jesus loves me, He is for me, and He has never been against me.

Satan has no rights over me. I break his power and every verbal agreement I have ever made with my words that have given the enemy license in my subconscious mind. I rebuke all power and authority he has over me and renounce these lies now. I am no longer bound by his chains, but I am free in Jesus. I am free because Jesus died on the cross for me, He paid the price for my sins. I repent of buying into Satan's lies and I turn from them now.

Jesus paid a high price for our freedom and instructed us not to be entangled again in the yoke of bondage. (Galatians 5:1, KJV) In Him every chain must fall. Visualize the chains, hear them coming off of you. In Him we are free to be who He created us to be. We are free to take dominion and authority, and every thought captive to the obedience of Christ. (2 Corinthians 10:5).

A friend of mine has written a book on prayer, called *The*

Kingdom Prayer Journal. In it, she walks you through prayers and teaches you to break agreements you have made with the enemy in your life through your spoken word. She walks you through how to renounce darkness in your life, your husband, your children's lives, and the lives of those you love. She has written out powerful prayers that are life-changing and powerful.

In *The Kingdom Prayer Journal,* she explains, "The enemy 'will trick you and tempt you by circumstances and situations that reinforce your hurt and fear of having these areas exposed to further pain. The root problem is the vulnerability of a damaged soul and its strongholds. Erected by a wounded soul to keep further pain out, these strongholds only succeed in keeping pain in and (Yahuah's) truth out' (*Shattering Your Strongholds* by Liberty S. Savard) We have been given the weapons (the keys of the kingdom) that demolish, destroy, and tear down strongholds, and the sword of the Spirit to vanquish the enemy, his demons, and his lies".

In Matthew 4 and in Luke 4 we see how Jesus Himself used the sword of the Spirit which is the Word of God to combat Satan. With each lie and promise the enemy brought before Him, Jesus retaliated by brandishing the sword of the Spirit, He used scripture to fight the enemy. Satan came in to tempt Jesus at His weakest point, after He had been without food and water for forty days in the wilderness. The devil comes at us and hits us when we are down. He does not fight fairly. Jesus finally dismissed Satan with the words, "Be gone, Satan!" (Matthew 4:10). He has given us that same authority through the power of His blood He shed for us at the cross. (See Appendix A for Ranalli's prayer on demolishing strongholds.)

A friend of mine experienced a terrible robbery in her own home. She and her husband are missionaries to Ecuador. Several men broke in, sprayed mace in her and her daughter's face, and took so much from her. She went through tremendous grieving as a result. She worked through her fears, but even well over a year to two after the robbery she has struggled. A friend of hers lamented, "When are you going to be back to yourself?" She confided to me that she would never be the same. Not that she won't know and experience joy again, but the robbery changed her. It changed things inside her. I cannot begin to fathom the plethora of emotions she has walked through as a result, but I do understand she is a different person now. After loss, we become stronger or weaker, but we are not left unchanged. We have a new normal. We are not the same person we were before the loss.

It seems that those that press into the Father with their heart and lives even when they are not going through storms of life are better able to turn to and rely on Him and let Him be their strength when their faith is severely tested. I have watched my friend emerge even stronger than she was before. She allowed herself to fully embrace and grieve her loss. One of her greatest things she lost was the content of a book she was writing, as well as years of homeschooling knowledge because they took her computer. She felt she lost much of her life's work. I respected and admired that she allowed herself to feel the full weight of her loss.

In this day and age, grief is often swept under the carpet. It takes a brave soul to face it head-on. I believe to be fully whole again; you do have to embrace it so that it loses it power over you.

A dear friend of mine, who was one of my college roommates, was an Art major. She recently taught me how she has experienced deep inner healing from Jesus. She said she starts out with asking the Lord to give her a heart to see, and a heart to hear. This is not talking about our mind, or even our ears to hear. We process things differently in our heart than in our minds. Numerous scriptures speak about the importance of our heart before the Lord, how He is concerned with our heart.

Then she asks Jesus, "Show me where I need to go, Jesus." She relayed a beautiful story with an experience she had with this. She said many people He leads to a place in their mind that is beautiful, but for her, He took her to a rocky cliff they were climbing together. He was walking before her holding her hand. Suddenly, she slipped and almost fell off the cliff. She was clinging to Jesus. She asked Him to show her what this vision meant, what she needed to know, and He showed her she had a trust issue. She asked Him to show her the root of it, where it came from, and He showed her its origin. Then He led her in healing her heart. Then He turned to her and she saw His face. As she cried, He softly kissed her face. It was intimate and precious.

Another time, Jesus showed her a lie she believed about herself that she wasn't good enough. She asked Him where this belief came from and He showed her an incident that happened between she and her father when she was a young girl. My friend had drawn a picture of a horse. It was the best she had ever done. She was so proud of it, and she took it to her dad to show him. He looked at it and told her that it was really good. He told her that if she drew it bigger, he would frame it, and put it on his wall. She drew it again, this time larger. When he looked at it, he said, "This one is not nearly as good as the first." She drew it again, and again, and again—nine or ten times. Her heart was deeply hurt and wounded by her dad.

When Jesus showed her this deep hurt, He rewrote the memory for her. She took her small drawing of the horse to Jesus to show Him. He was delighted in it. He took the picture, framed it, and put it on His wall!! He validated her and healed her heart.

He wants to bring us to wholeness. This is not the same as perfection. None of us will ever be perfect, and as a result, so many believe the Lord cannot use them to minister to others because they are not perfect. That is a lie of the enemy that keeps many people from walking in the purpose the Lord has for us. Each one of us has a purpose. He can use every heart; every life yielded to him. He can use us more fully if we are whole.

You may be like an onion, with layer upon layer to be peeled back. You may have bought into lies and untruths that hinder you from fulfilling your destiny. As the Lord reveals to you lies from the enemy you have believed, then renounce those lies, ask Him to show you how you should be thinking. There may be generational sins that are impacting your life that need to be identified and renounced. He wants to bring you to a place of wholeness and then use you to bring others into those same truths. Nothing you walk through is for no reason. He can use everything that ever happens in your life for His glory. It often seems that the worst things you walk through are those things that He uses for His greatest glory in your life.

Find scripture to confirm the truth He reveals to you. Memorize it, meditate on it, and stand on His promises for you. If you allow the Lord to lead you, He will take you through the healing you need in your heart. He may bring up memories long forgotten. No one knows you as He does, or loves you as deeply. He knows every single hurt you have experienced, and everything that can hinder you from being a dominant force for the Kingdom. The enemy wants you to believe his lies to render you ineffective in Kingdom work, Jesus wants to set you free to live as His son or daughter. You are made in His image. He rejoices over you.

I want to share something with you that can bring deep inner healing. To me, this was a healing balm even to read it. My 19-year-old nephew, Christian Fowler, who is a marvel to me, wrote it. It, like so many of his writings, is divinely inspired. Let it wash over you. Let it speak to, and soothe your soul.

"And Yahweh said,
I am He that initiated the first motion, of which all that is has come to be. I am He that will love, far beyond what you can comprehend or have learned. I am He of which much has been written, but that has

never been done justice. I am He that the earnest heart yearns for. I am He of which the strong heart has been made. I am He that has given of my own nature, that you have been given the gift to fight with me.

I am He that is zealous, jealous and alive. I am He that holds an armory greater than any conceived of elsewhere. I am He who dawns a sword forged of what cannot break. Unsheathed for those who will be won.

I am He that will win all. All that opposes me is of a different kind than that of which I am concerned. I am He who knows your heart intimately, beyond the tattered stains you believe are bound to it. I am He who sets conviction in your heart like the gems of heaven. I am He who supplies the grace of power.

I am He that dawns power. Unable to be dried up by your fires, unable to be quenched by your rivers, your wisdom is my foolishness. Your heart's laugh is my joy. I am He who is that of which you are derived; I am He unto which you will return.

I am He that romances. I am He that binds your heart to the ones around. I am He that is beyond what you imagined your treasure would be. For I am all that you love in this world. I am, of my design, the eyes of the ones you love and miss, the moments you yearn for. I am all of this; the gifts you have known and have not yet known. I am He that walks with you in your step. I am He that holds your hand. I am your anchor and shield; I am the wind in your sails, I am the song in your heart. All that your spirit longs for, of virtues and attributes, of events and occasion, of all that will come to pass that blesses any heart; all that has been laden in you of goodness and greatness, I am.

How long will you question who I am? Do I not speak loud enough? Do I leave space in your heart of which I cannot fill? Is your spirit foreign to its Father? Have I not given you fear of me to be alive? Is your very breath not a testament to my power? Have I not supplied you with more than enough to know who it is you belong to?

How long will you question who I am? I am Love. I am the beginning and the end. I am more than your present concerns, more long-suffering than your entire life. I Am that I Am.

I Am."

YOU WANT JOY?

"Only when life is seen as a gift and received with the open hands of gratitude is it the joy God meant for it to be."

John Claypool, *Tracks of a Fellow Struggler*

"Joy is the greatest cleanser, and it is the greatest testimony to our faith."

St. Francis of Assisi

I woke up this morning with a dream. In it, my husband Greg and I and our three youngest children were staying at a motel. While there, we had been working at a job. The first two days we had worked it together, and that night I had told Greg that for me it was "the job from hell." It wasn't even bad; it was just not what I wanted to be doing. I was at a desk, selling medical equipment and it was around some obsolete corner down a dark hallway. It was depressing and glum. In my dream, I had decided I was going to bug out of our third and final day on the

YOU WANT JOY?

job. I was going to take the kids and head home and leave it in my husband's more than capable hands. That morning we were talking, and he informed me that I needed to stay and work because he had things to tend to with his real business.

I broke out crying, almost sobbing. (This would not be my normal reaction.) Come to find out; it was 10:15 am, and I was supposed to be on the job at 9 am. Even Joy, who always pipes up that she will stay with me because she just likes to be with me, slipped away with her brothers so she would not get roped into staying. Greg clears his throat, like, "Aren't you going to kiss me?" I start to huff away, check my attitude (a little), head back to kiss him, and then he won't kiss me goodbye (which he always does).

I am groggy and just starting to wake up, and not wanting to because I am so unmotivated by the dream. I am hysterically crying all the way to the job. I start realizing as I am waking up, I can be the sunshine on this job. I can illuminate things. He is within me to do that. I can be a light. It is all in my perspective and my attitude. Greg rarely asks me to do something like this, and it is only for a day. I got this!

As I opened my eyes, I looked at the sunrise. It was the most glorious sunrise I had ever witnessed, and we have seen some beautiful ones here in Oklahoma! I leaped out of bed, grabbed my camera—ok, my phone, and took pictures. I texted Greg, who had already left the house, "Do you see this glorious sunrise?!" He responded, "Yes, just drove into it!! I figured that was

258

for me, but maybe God is smiling on you too, huh!!" He makes me laugh.

Greg reminded me of the gift the sunrise was for us this morning. On this same morning three years ago, Greg and I had the privilege of flying to Colorado and arriving at the hospital bed of our brain-dead son. His face was swollen and slightly disfigured from the gunshot wound, but he was still Luke. We got to spend his last twelve hours there with him, kissing on him, loving on him, saying our goodbyes and crying on his chest. It was a gift for which I am eternally grateful. We were there with him until they came to take him to the operating room so he could be an organ donor.

When we arrived at the hospital, our focus could have been our devastating loss. We could have gotten lost in the darkness of it all, focusing on the details of Luke putting the gun to his forehead and pulling the trigger. We could have gotten stuck on the "What if's…." or the "If only's…." Instead, our focus was on the incredible gift the Father opened up for us to be with him at his bedside for those final twelve hours of his on this earth. My nephew later told us there was no joy at all, no light in the room until we arrived. He said when we walked in, the whole demeanor of the room changed.

He then took me back to the dream I woke up with this morning. It is all in our perspective. He is always relentlessly pursuing us. It is up to us to be thankful, to respond in gratitude for His gifts. So many miss the gifts! We have had so many people tell us we are special as a family, but each of us is special in the eyes of the Lord. He loves every one of us immeasurably! We have had to walk through the most difficult experience of our lives, but in the midst, we have the eyes to see the myriad of ways He uses all the resources of Heaven to minister to us!!!

We miss the gifts when our focus is wrong. We only know His deepest joy through gratitude. That is why He is constantly reminding us to look for the good in everything. To thank Him IN all things. We can always find good in anything—so we can always know JOY.

I am reminded of a story Corrie Ten Boom tells in *The Hiding Place*. She and her sister are assigned to the worst barracks in the concentration camp. The fleas are so bad that the soldiers won't even go near to inspect the place. Her saint of a sister Betsy, who does not live to see their release, tells her they need to thank the Lord even for the fleas. Corrie is appalled at the very idea—the insects that are chewing holes in their skin and causing such great discomfort. She begins to thank the Lord even for the fleas.

Corrie and Betsy had been able to steal a Bible into the concentration camp and used it in their barracks to begin having what became a glorious Bible study among the hardened women in there with them. They later realized the liberty they had and the privilege of having the Bible study could only have happened because the soldiers were scared to come in their barracks because of the fleas! They saw God's goodness in even that. He uses everything.

He showed me how my perspective this morning in the dream changed when I chose to look for the good in my circumstances. We can always know joy because He is always within us. He will never leave us or forsake us. Our joy is not dependent on

> *Our joy is not dependent on our circumstances.*

our circumstances. We can do (or face) all things through Christ who strengthens us.

Mary Beth Chapman wrote a book, *Choosing to SEE*, after her son accidentally ran over and killed his six-year-old sister he adored. She talks about God using a butterfly to give her the eyes to see His goodness to them in carrying them through, as a family, the gravity of their loss. Her daughter loved butterflies, and that was the thing the Lord used to open her eyes.

We can choose to focus on our pain, or we can look for His gifts. We can number them, and thereby be intentional in recognizing them. Lots of friends of mine tell me they thank Him, but they don't journal or count them. It is incredible to go back and look at all the ways He met me in a particular season in my life. It reminds me of His love for me. This morning I was writing the 6,200th gift He had given me in my thankful journal. Over 6,000 ways He has shown me His love in the past few years! It has changed me. I never understood in my heart of hearts how much He really loved me, how much He loves each one of us before like I do now.

Several nights ago, Greg and I were in the hot tub, and I looked up and saw the entire sky above us, framed by the trees, had clouds that formed the face of a majestic lion. Wow! Jesus is the lion of the tribe of Judah. He is like Aslan, the Lion in *The*

Lion, the Witch, and the Wardrobe. He fights our battles for us. It was powerful! I made Greg move over to my side so he could see from my perspective what I was seeing. Then, he saw it too. Our perspective is huge. As we choose to embark on a journey of gratitude, of looking for Him in everything, He changes our perspective.

This morning I was sharing all this with my sister. She brought up another point. She and her husband have gone through years and years of financial struggles, where they had the privilege of having to trust the Lord for their every need. One day a friend of hers walked in and commented on the peace that was in my sister's home. She said she would not have been willing to pay the price my sister had to have that—the cost of having to learn to trust the Father completely. It is not because of the price we pay, it is because He is so there for us through it all.

We will all go through "stuff" in our lives. Are we willing to give it to the Lord and trust Him in the process? He is most concerned about the character He is developing in us so we become more and more like Him. Toni reminded me that in growing up Mom taught us you could never say, "No Lord", because if you are saying no, He is not truly your Lord. She and I both decided years ago that we are willing. Willing to allow the Lord to do whatever He chooses in and through us. He is always about using whatever happens in our life to make us stronger.

One incredible source of joy I have experienced is through Kat Kerr's teachings. I look her up on YouTube and listen to her. She has visited Heaven on numerous occasions. She tells her story about how for years and years she was awake at night between midnight and four, seeking God and knowing Him intimately. One day in 1998, she says Jesus walked through the wall of her living room and told her they (the Father, Son, and Holy Spirit) wanted to begin taking her on visits to Heaven because they wanted her to come back and share with people about Heaven.

She teaches revelation the Father reveals to her. She said the three things that matter the most in our time and life here on earth are:

1. Worship—loving Him
2. Loving others
3. Prayer

She says, "They are all weapons. When you are worshipping in the spirit realm you are creating a masterpiece with your love. It is like ribbons of tapestry. In Heaven, you have a Praise Gallery gathering everything you created. For intercessors who stood in the gap, angels collect your worship, and it becomes like liquid gold." She goes on to say, "If you are being crushed, stand up and worship with everything in you."

Our Heavenly Father, who designed the universe and all that is in it, who is your very breath and source of life, has created you with a God-sized hole in your heart for Him. It is written into your very DNA. Can you imagine if you had to consciously think to take every breath? Or if you had to be in charge of causing your heart to beat? Our bodies are the most unfathomable miracle. This same Father who so intimately fashioned you in your mother's womb loves you so deeply. The very hairs of your head are numbered. Have you ever been in an airplane looking down and become overwhelmed with how vast even our world is? And to think He knows and cares about every thought that passes through your mind!

And how vast are His thoughts toward you? If you were to number them, they would outnumber the sands in the sea! Your Heavenly Father adores you. He loves you and delights in you! The Lord joys in you!! He wants to fill you with His joy as you thank Him in all things.

Zephaniah 3:17 says, "The Lord your God is in the midst of you, a Mighty one, a Savior—Who saves! He will rejoice over you with joy; He will rest (in silent satisfaction), and in His love, He will be silent and make no mention (of past sins, or even recall them); He will exult over you with singing." Can you picture that? See Him rejoicing over you with joy, exulting over you with singing! Your Abba Father, who created the universe, the galaxies and all that are in them, who produced over 300 varieties of beetles alone, who designed your miraculously functioning body, rejoices over you with joy and singing!!!

The only way we can know deep joy is to know Jesus. Worship unlocks joy. It does not matter whether we are worshipping, or playing worship music. It all matters! Worship dispels darkness. It breaks up the forces of darkness in the spirit realm. It ushers in joy. Many Christians are not walking in joy. Our joy should set us apart. We should radiate His joy. When you walk into a room, others should feel Jesus because of His presence in you.

I find after listening to Kat Kerr's teaching, and revelation on Heaven, that I rejoice in my son's being there ahead of me. That is what I am living life for – to know the Father and to make Him known. Luke is already there with Him. Early on in this book, I mentioned Jesus telling my son's friend that, no, he wasn't going to come back, but it was not before Jesus asked Luke if he wanted to come back. Kat Kerr says your loved one would be crazy to want to come back. Heaven is phenomenal! It is the most excellent adventure of all! She shares things she has seen there, and what we have to joy in and look forward to, and how the Father wants us to live out our lives now in what she calls the Kingdom Age. She calls it that because she says the Father calls it that. I eagerly anticipate Heaven, and that makes living life to the fullest here and now all the more beautiful!

You want Joy? "Let gratitude be your source of joy." "Joy is the surest sign of the presence of God." Thank Him in all things. Choose to look for Him in everything. Choose to focus your mind on the good, the kind, the pure, the true, the honest, the just, and the lovely. Think on these things.

A friend of mine, Lynne, recently told me when she was growing up her dad said to her, "You can either be a positive or a negative person in life. Being positive is a lot more fun." She took his advice and she is a delightful person to be around. She looks for the good. Negative people can be draining to be around; positive people energize others. She has become a person who sees the glass as half full rather than half empty.

I keep these three scriptures on my bathroom mirror:

Psalms 16:11 You will show me the path of life; in Your Presence is fullness of joy, at your right hand there are pleasures forevermore.

Acts 2:28 You have made known to me the ways of life; You will enrapture me, (diffusing my soul with joy) with and in Your Presence.

Acts 13:52 The disciples were continually diffused (throughout their souls) with joy and the Holy Spirit.

I love the verse, "A man hath joy by the answer of his mouth, and a word spoken in due season, how good is it!" (Proverbs 15:23) Our joy comes from what comes out of our mouth, and what comes out of our mouth is from within us. Joy comes from within.

St. Francis of Assisi lived 1182–1226 A. D. He referred to the Father as, 'The Holy.' That is beautiful.

I love this poem he wrote that shows how the Father loves, adores, and joys in us:

God Would Kneel Down

I think God might be a little prejudiced. For once He asked me to join Him on a walk through this world,

And we gazed into every heart on this earth, and I noticed He lingered a bit longer before any face that was weeping,

And before any eyes that were laughing,

And sometimes when we passed a soul in worship, God too would kneel down.

I have come to learn: God adores His creation.

∽

He also wrote, "Yes, I will console any creature before me that is not laughing or full of passion for their art or life; for laughing and passion – beauty and joy – is our heart's truth, all else is labor and foreign to the soul."

Beauty and passion are our true north. Our Jesus wants us to walk in joy.

His message, from His word, "Shine—be radiant with the glory of the Lord, for your light is come, and the glory of the Lord is risen upon you!" Isaiah 60: 1b "To grant (consolation and joy) to those who mourn in Zion, to give them an ornament—a garland or diadem—of beauty instead of ashes, the oil of joy for mourning, the garment (expressive) of praise instead of a heavy, burdened and failing spirit; that they may be called oaks of righteousness (lofty, strong and magnificent, distinguished for uprightness, justice and right standing with God), the planting of the Lord, that He may be glorified." Isaiah 61:3 As we shine for Him, as we walk in the joy of the Lord, as we *fully* live, He is glorified in us!

We glorify Him by walking in joy. "I will greatly rejoice in the Lord; my soul shall exult in my God!" Isaiah 61: 10a

Our own words determine if we have joy. The condition of our hearts will determine if we have joy. Our joy is not dependent on our circumstances; it is not an outward thing, it is what is inward. Joy is found in the presence of the Lord and in and through gratitude and thankful hearts – regardless of what is happening about us. If you have not yet begun your thankful journal, begin it today. It will be the start of the most amazing, eye-opening, joy-filled adventure for you! Let it transform you. Let gratitude fill your soul with joy!

APPENDIX A

DEMOLISH STRONGHOLDS

Abba, you have given me weapons that have divine power to demolish strongholds (2 Corinthians 10:5). So, in the name of Yahushuah, and in the authority you have given me, I demolish and destroy every stronghold – every pretense, imagination, and thought in _____ that sets itself up against the knowledge and truth of Yahuah. I demolish all strongholds of pride, intellect, logic, reasoning, justification, defensiveness, timidity, and denial in _____ that sets itself up against the knowledge and truth of Yahuah.

Abba, You have said that you have given me the keys of the kingdom of Heaven… and whatever I loose (cut off, destroy) on earth will be as it is already loosed in Heaven (Matthew 6:19). You have commanded us to break every yoke and so in the name of Yahushuah and in the authority You have given me…

*I destroy and loose every generational, verbal, spiritual, soulish, and physical yoke over _____.

*I loose and cast our all sickness and their causes, every unclean thing (including allergies, toxins, heavy metals, virus, bacteria, parasite, fungus and amoeba) from _____ body.

*I loose, destroy, and expose all unrighteous wrong soul ties, wrong inordinate relationships, or intimidating and fraudulent influences from _____.

*I loose the power, guilt, and effects of any wrong words, verbal agreements, accusations, gossip, lies, rash vows, and harsh or careless words spoken by _____.

*I loose every wrong, unrighteous thought, pattern of thinking, attitude, and idea from _____'s mind.

*I loose the power and effects of deceptions and lies from _____.

*I loose every wrong unrighteous feeling and emotion – including all fear, anger, timidity, rejection, pain, confusion, discouragement, jealousy, hate, and shame from _____.

*I loose all unrighteous desires, motives, and behaviors. I loose all lust, fear, neediness, selfishness, greed, pride, and envy; all compulsive, rigid, divisive, timid, and religious behaviors from _____.

I loose the spirit and power of religion, the fear of man, the fear of failure, the fear of death, and the love of the world: the lust of the flesh, the lust of the eyes, and the pride of life from _____.

*I loose and destroy all of these oppressions, strongholds, bondages, and yokes in the name and authority of Yahush-uah – because HIS BLOOD IS ENOUGH to set _____ free from every bondage!

Endnotes

Nobody Ever Died from Marijuana

"Death changes us, the living. In the presence of death, we become more aware of life. It can inspire us to decide what really matters in life – and then to seek it." (Candy Lightner, *Giving Sorrow Words,* Grand Central Publishing, Warner Books, 1991).

Movie "*Flight*", director Robert Zemeckis, writer John Gatins, starring Denzel Washington, 2012.

Luke

Bobby Petrocelli, *Triumph Over Tragedy (*Waco, TX: WRS Publishing, 1995).

Bobby Petrocelli, *You Matter, It Doesn't* (Sapulpa, OK: Honor-Net Publishers, 2015).
Tim McGraw, "Live Like Your Dying", song, 1997.

Ann Voskamp, *One Thousand Gifts* (Grand Rapids, MI: Zondervan, 2010).

GRIEVING IS NOT OPTIONAL

"Grief denied is grief unhealed." (Barbara Bartocci, *Nobody's Child Anymore*, Sorin Books, 2000).

Dr. Bradly Nelson, *The Emotion Code* (Mesquite, NV: Wellness Unmasked Publishing, 2007).

Jerry Sitter, *A Grace Disguised* (Grand Rapids, MI: Zondervan, 1995, 2004), 101, 73.

CHOOSING THANKFULNESS

Ann Voskamp, *One Thousand Gifts.*

James Strong, *Strong's Concordance* (Peabody, MA: Hendrickson Publishing).

Ann Voskamp, *One Thousand Gifts, p. 176, 113.*

TV show, "Touched by an Angel", creator John Masius, starring Roma Downey, John Dye, Della Reese, 1994–2003.

John Claypool, *Tracks of a Fellow Struggler* (Harrisburg, NY: Morehouse Publishing, 1995, revised 2004), p. 65.

Sarah Young, *Jesus Calling* (Nashville, TN: Thomas Nelson, 2004), p. 236.

Kat Kerr, You Tube, "Angels", 2:28:32, July 17, 2018

NAVIGATING THROUGH GRIEF

"It is important for us not to deny our pain, and take time to mouth our losses. Without giving ourselves time to grieve, our wounds may never heal." Rebecca Wagner Systema, article.

Kenneth Haugk, *Journeying Through Grief* (St. Louis, MO: Stephens Ministries, 2004).

"Jesus Loves Me, He is for Me", Chris Tomlin. Copyright 2014 9t One Songs, Ariose Music, Hillsong Music Publishing, S. D. G. Publishing, Sixsteps Songs, Worship Together Music, (Administrators Capitol CMG Publishing).

Jace Goodman, "11 months", Reddit, Best of Reddit, 2016. Used by permission.

Jerry Sitter, *Grace Disguised.*

Ann Voskamp, *One Thousand Gifts,* p. 105, 106.

GRACE TO GRIEVE

Francis Roberts, *Come Away My Beloved* (Ojai, CA: The King's Press, 1970), p. 126.

"Reckless Love", Cory Asbury. Published Jan 19, 2018 by Bethel Music (Sound recordings); Adorando Publishing, Bethel Music (Publishing), ASCAP, and 9 Music Rights Societies.

Ann Voskamp, *One Thousand Gifts, p. 97, 33.*

Francis Roberts, *Come Away My Beloved, p. 56.*

"Blessed Be Your Name, Matt Redman, 2002. Recorded in Atlanta, Georgia, from album "Where Angels Fear to Tread", Capitol Christian Music Group.

Voskamp, p. 120-121.

"We are healed of a suffering only by experiencing it in full." Marcel Proust, quoted by Haugk in *Experiencing Grief, Book 2* of Journeying Through Grief Series, p. 6.

Kenneth Haugk, *Experiencing Grief, Journeying through Grief, Book 2 (St. Louis, MO: Stephens Ministries, 2004), p. 4, 9, 10.*

"Perhaps the most important truth I have learned is that healing is heart-based, not head-based." Alan Wolfelt, *Understanding Your Grief,* quoted in Haugk, *Experiencing Grief,* Book 2 of the Journeying through Grief series, p. 4.

"We shall steer safely through every storm, so long as our heart is right, our intention fervent, our courage steadfast, and our trust fixed on God." St. Francis de Sales, quoted in:

In the Shelter of His Wings, (Cookeville, TN: Harvest House Publishers, 2004), p. 61.

"Every person who truly, deeply shares the pain of your grief with you is doing God's work." Haugk, *A Time to Grieve, Book 1,* Journeying Through Grief Series, p.41

"Stand still and whisper God's name. He is closer than you think." Max Lucado, quoted in Journeying through Grief Series, Book 1, p. 41

"Soul-full people love. If people want their souls to grow through loss, they must eventually decide to love even more than they did before." Sitter, p. 183–184

"Spend the whole of your one wild and beautiful life investing in many lives, and God simply will not be outdone." Voskamp, p. 197

"Joy emerges from the ashes of your adversity through trust and thankfulness." Young, p. 301

"My depths are held by peace. The surface may be disturbed, it's the depths that count." Stanley Jones, quoted in: *In the Shelter of His Wings, p.44.*

"His joy springs forth most abundantly in souls that have been soaked in tears." Roberts, p. 109.

"Rejoice in the One who understands you completely and loves you perfectly." Young, p. 80.

Being Intentional in Your Thought Life

Rebecca Stringer, *Within Heaven's Gates* (New Kinsington, PA: Whitaker House, 1984).

Debi Pearl, *Created to Be His Help Meet* (Pleasantville, TN: No Greater Joy Ministries, 2004).

Deep Inner Healing

"What we have once enjoyed and deeply loved we can never lose, for all that we love deeply becomes a part of us." Helen Keller, quoted in *Rebuilding and Remembering, Book 4,* in the Journeying Through Grief Series, by Haugk, p. 33.

R. W. Ranalli, *The Kingdom Prayer Journal, p. 58, 59. (*Can only be purchased at this time on Lulu.com.http://www.lulu.com/. shop/rw-ranalli/the-kingdom-prayer-journal/.paperback/.prod-uct-23246405.html)

Liberty S. Savard, *Shattering Your Strongholds (Newberry, FL: Bridge Logos, 1993*, p. 29.

YOU WANT JOY?

John Claypool, *Tracks of a Fellow Struggler, p. 63.*

"Joy is the greatest cleanser, and it is the greatest testimony to our faith." St Francis of Assisi, quoted in: Daniel Ladinsky, *Love Poems from God (*New York, New York: Penguin Compass, 2002), p, 34

Corrie Ten Boom, *The Hiding Place* (Random House, 1982.)

Mary Beth Chapman, *Choosing to SEE (Grand Rapids, MI: Revell, 2010).*

St Francis of Assisi: Daniel Ladinsky, *Love Poems from God, P. 41, 45.*

APPENDIX A

Ranalli, p. 36–38. Used by permission.

A Final Word...

Many of you have been given this book by someone who has cared for you in your time of loss. You may know others whose lives can be impacted by this message as well.

Pay it forward discount: For every ten copies you purchase directly from the author, you receive one free copy. Simply contact us using the e-mail address below.

To purchase bulk copies of this book, email us at:
GraceinGrief7@gmail.com

To contact author or for speaking engagements:
GraceinGrief7@gmail.com

Ten percent (10%) of the proceeds from the sale of this book will be used to bring grace to others in their time of grief and loss.